17⁰⁰

GOD'S TIMETABLE FOR A TROUBLED WORLD

God's Timetable
For A Troubled World

Investigating End Time Events

Donald C. B. Cameron
BTh, MA, PhD

Foreword by Tom Wilson

JOHN RITCHIE LTD
CHRISTIAN PUBLICATIONS

40 Beansburn, Kilmarnock, Scotland

ISBN-13: 978 1 907731 49 5

Copyright © 2012 by John Ritchie Ltd.
40 Beansburn, Kilmarnock, Scotland

www.ritchiechristianmedia.co.uk

Typeset by John Ritchie Ltd., Kilmarnock
Printed by Bell & Bain Ltd., Glasgow

Contents

Foreword

When the Lord Jesus met the assembled witnesses to His resurrection, He spoke to them of God's timetable for the baptism of the Spirit, and they inquired of God's timetable for the restoration of the kingdom to Israel, Acts 1:5, 6. He left no doubts in their minds that God had a timetable for both events. The first event would occur "not many days hence"; the second was as certain as the first but the Father would not reveal to them His timetable. Graciously He assured them that the timetable of future events including Israel's restoration was under divine control. God would not be taken by surprise, nor would He be found wanting as He implemented His timetable.

Over the subsequent four decades, the New Testament writings recorded much the Lord Himself had taught about the future, and by the Spirit apostles John, Paul and Peter penned letters which developed prophetic themes in respect of Israel and the Church. None of them sought to calculate when the Lord would come. The "faith … once delivered to the saints" has therefore always included predictive prophecy, and in that faith every Christian requires to be grounded.

The Publishers' exercise to make available a relatively short volume aimed at those untaught in, or unsure about, God's timetable is to be welcomed. The author has endeavoured to address the needs of a readership who may never have studied what God has revealed about the future. Candidly he has addressed his intended audience with clarity, dealing with the range of fears that are gripping the many minds. He does not add to the growing list of worries about wars and rumours of wars, about earth's resources and economic ills. *God's Timetable for a Troubled World* neither offers predictions based on science, nor speculation about the unknown but sets out what every man and woman should know about the future as God has revealed it. The author also points to the Saviour God has provided as the only assurance for the future God has prepared for those who love Him.

Tom Wilson

Professor Thomas Wilson, Formerly Editor of *Believer's Magazine* and What The Bible Teaches New Testament series.

CHAPTER ONE

By God Revealed –
By Churches Concealed

OUT-OF-DATE?

Do you find the words "By churches concealed" provocative or disturbing? If your local Church has all the answers to people's concerns about the future of the world and society, then go there and forget about this book. If not, please read on.

This is no introduction to one of the modern cults. They claim to know what is going on, taking full advantage of widespread ignorance within mainstream Christianity, at a time when the world is becoming desperate for trustworthy and authoritative answers. Each cult tells something quite different from the others. Nothing in this little book can be regarded as heretical or cultish; but it does deal in some depth with the neglected, the overlooked, the forgotten, the trivialised and the studiously ignored. The Bible does not answer all our questions nor does it satisfy idle curiosity, but it does tell us all that we need to know, and much more than many people suspect.

This is my sixth book and one of the shortest. Some of the previous ones have assumed of its readers some familiarity with the Bible and with prophecy. However I have been asked by several people to write for thoughtful people who are not familiar with the Bible, and for those who come from churches which never talk about what the Bible reveals about the future of our planet. I count it a privilege to write for them. A Brief Glossary of Essential Terms is included at the end of the book for those unfamiliar with Bible terminology. In some respects this book will be out of date by the time it is printed, so quickly is the world moving from crisis to crisis. National leaders are beginning to panic. So why bother writing it? Why bother reading it? For the simple reason that it deals chiefly with non-negotiable truths concerning the near and distant future of this planet and the human race.

Even during the short time that this book has taken to write and edit, storm clouds have continued to gather. Doom and gloom are forecast in economics, politics, the environment, employment and the very moral fabric of society. The Middle East is becoming ever more volatile, with alliances and power blocs continually changing shape. War is imminent say some analysts. However the most decisive factor of all is usually forgotten, even by Christians; God is still sovereign. His timetable will not be thwarted by political manoeuvring and national ambitions. One day He will cause all wars to cease, but not until many other necessary things have been accomplished. Wars must come, but only within His permissive will.

SEVEN REASONS TO STUDY BIBLE PROPHECY
Investigating end-time prophecy is not the believer's first priority, but ignoring it deprives us of a significant God-given resource. Comparing the Bible's predictive prophecy with what is happening in today's world is no fringe activity for specialists or eccentrics. It provides:-

1. Eloquent testimony to the divine inspiration of the Bible.
2. Reassurance to believers that God's plans are still on track.

3. A challenge to those who have never faced up to the need to get right with their Creator.

4. A warning to those who have been challenged not to delay.

5. A wake-up call to reluctant churches to study and to preach prophecy in addition to their other important activities.

6. A reminder that this age could end at any moment and a short traumatic one begin before the world is put to rights.

7. A call for those of us already convinced and committed to live lives worthy of our calling as believers.

The Lord Jesus Christ Himself is the greatest prophet of all. He is central to so much prophecy in both His First and Second Comings. His Olivet Discourse is found in three of the four Gospels. The last book of the Bible is: *"The Revelation of Jesus Christ, which God gave unto him, to shew unto his servants things which must shortly come to pass"* (Revelation 1:1). The Bible closes with His full title: *"He which testifieth these things saith, Surely I come quickly. Amen. Even so, come, Lord Jesus. The grace of our Lord Jesus Christ be with you all. Amen"* (Revelation 22:20-21). In this book we will not always call him the Lord Jesus Christ – after all, the New Testament doesn't. If we are believers - believers in Him – we call ourselves 'Christians' not 'Jesus People'. He is our Lord. 'Christ' is the Greek form of the Hebrew 'Messiah', meaning Anointed, and we may use this name more in the Millennial prophecies, for instance. 'Jesus' is the Latinised form of the Hebrew, which we usually use, for 'Saviour': *"Thou shalt call his name JESUS: for he shall save his people from their sins"* (Matthew 1:21). It was given to Him only when He humbled Himself and became man. We may sometimes be flexible in our use of these names, but should never forget their significance.

WHY MANY CHURCHES KEEP SILENT

Some well-meaning people think that perhaps God can be persuaded to change His mind about what He has foretold. We concede that there are many instances where prayer changes things, and certainly God wants us to make our requests known to Him. However some things are presented in the Bible as being negotiable, while others are not. The outline prophetic programme is presented as being non-negotiable. Were it negotiable, we would effectively be able to amend God's revealed plans for dealing with rebellion and lawlessness in this world; we could even deny the Lord Jesus Christ His right one day to be recognised and acclaimed in the world where He was once rejected and crucified. Some matters are much, much safer in God's hands.

God was very strict in Old Testament times with religious leaders who insisted that prophets should announce only good news, when God had, for very good reasons, commissioned them to preach bad news. Examples can be found in I Kings 22:7-28, Isaiah 30:9-10, Jeremiah 23:16-29, Ezekiel 13:1-16; Scripture does not conceal the sheer frustration which these faithful souls felt at being portrayed as 'doom and gloom merchants', when they were simply obeying God. In Isaiah such refusal to listen to God's severe words is described as rebelliousness. Things are little different today. Some insist on bright prospects just round the corner, whilst others simply keep quiet about the bad side of the news, and yet others preach the bad side without proclaiming that ultimately, following Christ's return, there will be a golden age right here. With such mixed messages, what are outsiders to think?

Believing God's graciously revealed plans is hardly likely to win us popularity contests in the politically correct amorphous mass of half-hearted nominal Christianity. But it does humbly acknowledge one of the loveliest privileges believers may enjoy, though some scornfully reject: *"Henceforth I call you not servants; for the servant knoweth not what his lord doeth: but I have called you friends; for all things that I have heard of my Father I have made known unto you"* (John 15:15). A little initial faith or even a preparedness to take prophecy seriously will be amply vindicated and rewarded as we see the whole wonderful plan emerge.

Perhaps some stay clear of studying end-time prophecy because some of the cults have tried to make it their province. But that is hardly an excuse for abandoning it to their tender mercies! The Millennium of the J.W. cult is far removed from ours, as indeed is their fatalistic philosophy that, because Armageddon is drawing near, there is no point in taking on traditional social responsibilities. A balance must be drawn between, on the one hand, unjustified optimism for a 'brave new world' before God intervenes spectacularly, and, on the other hand, a pessimism which says that there is nothing whatsoever that we can do in the meantime except preach the Gospel.

The Bible tells us *how* the **world** will end, and has a lot to say about what will happen *before* the world ends. But it does not tell us *when* the world will end. The Bible also tells us how this **age** will end and has a lot to say about what will happen next, but it does not tell us exactly when it will end, though it does gives important signs to keep us on our toes. The end of the age can never be pinpointed by mystical codes or cabalistic calculations. The important distinction between 'age' and 'world' is all too often blurred.

In due course we will distinguish between the end of the age and the end of the world. We will demonstrate that the end of this **age** could come upon us very suddenly, but that the end of the **world** cannot occur within the next thousand years. We will in due course define what we mean by the end of the age, and discover that it will be dramatic, and for many traumatic in the extreme.

Prophecy occupies a great deal of space in both the Old and New Testament. One of the last sermons Jesus preached before His crucifixion and the first one afterwards were prophetic in nature. Why? Without an understanding of God's revealed plans, we are unable fully to comprehend God's purposes in history, we miss one of the most powerful tools for evangelism and one of the most potent incentives for holy living. I have good friends, sincere believers, whose public prayers can only confuse their earthly hearers by asking for things now, which in the prophetic timetable are impossible. The problem is that they have only the haziest idea of this timetable.

Thus we have the sad situation, where most churches have nothing authoritative to say to a panic stricken world about what is to happen on this planet before Christ returns in power. Satan hates attention being drawn to his coming defeat and doom. Where he can he discourages interest; if this fails he distorts truths. Thus, as a generalisation, we might say that in Britain and Europe he is currently fairly successful in discouraging study, whilst on the other side of the Atlantic, where interest is much greater, he makes more use of the cults and diversions; also that dreadful mainly Transatlantic phenomenon called the Prosperity Gospel, which demeans those who are called upon in this life to endure hardship for their Lord, abounds in the U.S.A. Sometimes over-zealous enthusiasts can play into his hands by insisting on trying to dot all the I's and crossing all the T's in the prophetic timetable, to the extent of making premature positive identifications of "actors about to appear on the end-time stage". When, as has happened, such "actors" suddenly die or disappear, cynics tend to assume that their entire programmes are flawed. The Bible tells us a great deal about the end-time programme, but leaves certain matters to be understood only by those actually experiencing them.

BIBLE VERSIONS USED
Sometimes passages will be quoted in full. Usually the 1611 Authorised Version (A.V.), called the King James Version in the U.S.A., will be used, unless indicated. This may take a little getting used to for some; but I will be quoting extensively to save readers constantly having to turn to the pages of Scripture. The A.V. does away with the problem of copyright. If you do have an A.V. Bible, please note that the chapter and page headings have been added and are not part of Holy Scripture. Some headings in prophetic passages in the A.V. are quite inappropriate.

No translation can be perfect. I have taught and interpreted Russian professionally, and know how difficult it is in any language to get the best balance between conveying the sense accurately and making a translation easily comprehensible. Some Bible versions stay as close to the original Hebrew and Greek as is reasonable; this is undoubtedly the best kind of translation for serious study, and I shall therefore use the New King James (N.K.J.V.), the John Nelson Darby (J.N.D.) and occasionally other versions such as the Revised Standard Version (R.S.V), when the sense seems to be more accurately presented there than in the A.V. I prefer to avoid the popular paraphrased versions, which may appeal to younger readers in particular by being very up-to-date in style. Some may be all very well for light reading, but are much more subject to the whims of their compilers, and may at times be positively misleading.

Before proceeding further, I would like to ask and answer some questions and to make some general observations.

WHAT IS PROPHECY?

Sometimes the word prophecy simply means preaching or proclaiming, but much more often it implies prediction or telling the future. The Bible contains a vast amount of this predictive prophecy. It is there for practical purposes and not for our entertainment; inevitably some prophecies will be debatable until their fulfilment draws near. Some of it is easy to understand and some is more difficult. Sometimes it comes in the form of visions; occasionally these visions are actually interpreted on the spot. Scenes in Heaven are described in a way to help us understand their significance, but are at present so far removed from our experience that we may well be baffled by what we are told. But much is in plain language and concerns future happenings on earth. Often two or more prophecies have to be compared to confirm the true sense. Sometimes answers come only through diligent and prayerful enquiry.

Those theologians who do not believe in the inspiration of the Holy Scriptures have used various ploys to discredit prophecies which would otherwise be very challenging and inconvenient for them. One trick is to try to prove that some of the Old Testament prophets actually lived and wrote after the events foretold; the books of Isaiah and Daniel have been prime targets. Invariably proof has been unearthed to vindicate the prophet's historicity and divinely imparted foreknowledge.

People whom we call Preterists assume that the significance of Bible prophecy ended during the First Century with the sack of Jerusalem by the Romans in 70 A.D. This is strange in view of the fact that the last book of the Bible, Revelation, was not written until well after this event. Moreover when Jesus did predict this fall of Jerusalem, He said that it would be the **beginning** of a new Jewish exile, not the **end**, which would occur many centuries later.

Some people assume that prophecy is only about what happens after we die; some of course is, but most is about what is still to happen on earth. Jesus spoke very severely to religious leaders and even to disciples who failed to recognise prophecy being fulfilled around them. *"When it is evening, ye say, It will be fair weather: for the sky is red. And in the morning, It will be foul weather today: for the sky is red and lowring. O ye hypocrites, ye can discern the face of the sky; but can ye not discern the signs of the times?"* (Matthew 16:2-3). Jesus was addressing both liberal and conservative religious leaders on this occasion. History repeats itself as we approach the time of *"men fainting with fear and with foreboding of what is coming on the world; for the powers of the heavens will be shaken"* (Luke 21:26 RSV).

FALSE PROPHETS
Periodically even mainstream Christians have been guilty of claiming 'inside' knowledge and being able to predict the date of the end of the age or of the world. If they truly believed the Bible, they would know very well that nobody knows when the end-time programme (and there is such a programme) is to start. Most of these date fixers are what we would call false prophets, but some have been sincere and genuine believers. Either way, they cause immense harm, because, like the shepherd boy in Aesop's Fable who cried "Wolf!" once too often, they have turned an immensely serious topic into a joke.

What I believe we can say quite categorically from the Bible is that, whatever else happens, the world is not going to end within the next thousand years, although this age (the Christian or Church Age) could end at any time. And what then? That is what we must find out, because it intimately affects every one of us.

WORSE BEFORE BETTER

There is nothing strange about the current lack of interest among the majority of church leaders. *"Be mindful of the words which were spoken before by the holy prophets, and of the commandment of us the apostles of the Lord and Saviour: knowing this first, that there shall come in the last days scoffers, walking after their own lusts, and saying, Where is the promise of his coming? for since the fathers fell asleep, all things continue as they were from the beginning of the creation"* (II Peter 3:2-4). What is significant is that Peter's prophecy is not about atheists or agnostics, but about people who believe in creation. Whilst Christianity is spreading like wildfire in lands where persecution and opposition is rife, in traditionally Christian lands it is being eroded, with every kind of compromise of Biblical standards being applauded as 'progressive'.

The drop in moral standards in countries which were generally considered to be Christian is a clear indicator that this age is drawing rapidly to a close. *"Now the Spirit speaketh expressly, that in the latter times some shall depart from the faith, giving heed to seducing spirits, and doctrines of devils; speaking lies in hypocrisy; having their conscience seared with a hot iron; forbidding to marry, and commanding to abstain from meats, which God hath created to be received with thanksgiving of them which believe and know the truth"* (I Timothy 4:1-3). *"For the time will come when they will not endure sound doctrine; but after their own lusts shall they heap to themselves teachers, having itching ears; and they shall turn away their ears from the truth, and shall be turned unto fables"* (II Timothy 4:3).

Apathy was prevalent at Jesus' first coming. If you know the Christmas story, you will recall what happened when wise men or *magi* from the East came to Herod, the upstart king of Judea, to enquire of him. Matthew 2:1-12 relates the whole incident. The religious leaders, who actually knew that the answer was Bethlehem, as foretold by Micah, simply were not interested in joining the wise men. They preferred their status quo to any unwelcome intervention on the part of God. And so it is today with all too many Christian leaders. Both generations have ignored the responsibility which comes with leadership; ultimately God will hold them responsible.

Please do not take this as wholesale criticism of all churches. Certainly some have departed so far from Christianity, as described in Acts and the following epistles or letters, that they are not truly Christian at all. But many others are doing a moderately or even very good job, preaching the Gospel, honouring God's commandments, caring in the community and showing a good example in a society which forgets that almost all long established charities were once Christian based. What, however, all too many suffer from is the condition described by Jesus on the evening of His resurrection day to His two distraught disciples. They were preoccupied by Jesus' crucifixion and death and unaware of the stupendous events of that day: *"Then he said unto them, O fools, and slow of heart to believe all that the prophets have spoken: Ought not Christ to have suffered these things, and to enter into his glory? And beginning at Moses and all the prophets, he expounded unto them in all the scriptures the things concerning himself."* (Luke 24:25-27). You will find the whole episode recorded in Luke 24:13-33. **Were more Christians prepared to compare** *"all that the prophets have spoken"* **with what is happening in today's world, people might be less despondent, more ready for their Lord's return, and would be considered to be more credible and relevant in an**

increasingly bewildered world. This is the main them of my book, 'Christian Credibility In A Global Crisis'.

Much mischief is done by failure to distinguish between the end of the world and the end of the age. The result is confusion, which sometimes leads to profitable exploration, but more often to people switching off. If there is nothing between these two momentous points, there is in theory little to study. Yet the Bible devotes much space to this important interval, which makes a great deal of sense of what so many fail to understand. We will devote much of this book to examining this interval.

MESSIANIC PROPHECIES
We will often refer to O.T. and N.T., rather than writing Old Testament and New Testament in full each time. Now O.T. prophecy was spread over a period from approximately 2,000 to 400 BC, starting early in the book of Genesis. Fifteen of the last seventeen O.T. books written between approximately 850 and 400 BC contain much more prophecy than all the others; Lamentations and Jonah are the two exceptions. Many of the Psalms also have significant prophecies.

It might be assumed that all the O.T. prophecies are now obsolete having been fulfilled, but that is a fallacy. Certainly some were fulfilled not long after their utterance, even occasionally on the same day; others were fulfilled later but within O.T. history, and yet others during the lifetime of Jesus, while others still await fulfilment. Those which are to be fulfilled after the end of the O.T period are generally Messianic. It has been calculated that around 330 of these were fulfilled at Jesus' first coming. Many O.T. prophecies skip over the entire Church Age, which started in the Acts of the Apostles. The fact that the Messiah is both God and Man was not understood formerly, despite there being much implicit evidence; this becomes so much more obvious seen with hindsight.

O.T. Messianic prophecies can be broadly divided into three categories, although some cover two or even three of these:

1. First Coming, to be born, to minister, to suffer, to die, to be resurrected and to ascend. We may sometimes refer to these, but will be concentrating on the future.
2. Tribulation or Day of Vengeance (we will define the terms later), concerning events up to and including His glorious return in power.
3. Millennial – these are numerous in the O.T. and there are several short ones in the Gospels, although the thousand year duration is not given until almost the last chapter of the Bible.

There is a quite illogical and very damaging assumption that O.T. prophecies already fulfilled in the New Testament can be taken literally, but that prophecies in either part of the Bible which concern what is still future should be taken figuratively or allegorically. Some of the easily understood O.T. prophecies foretelling Jesus' First Coming are well known. Here are a few examples:-

Micah 5:2 & Matthew 2:1	Jesus' birthplace in Bethlehem Judah
Isaiah 7:14 & Matthew 1:18	Jesus born of a virgin
Isaiah 53:3 & John 1:11	Jesus rejected by His own people and accepted by others
Zechariah 9:9 & John:12:13-15	Jesus' kingly yet humble arrival at Jerusalem on a donkey
Isaiah 53:12 & Luke 23:33	Jesus crucified alongside criminals

People in Old Testament times knew that God had promised to send a Messiah but were puzzled by the stark contrasts between such mild prophecies as those above and others of a judgmental nature and yet others of a righteous kingdom. Some rabbis or teachers tried to get over the problem by assuming that there were to be two Messiahs, a suffering one and a triumphant one. With the benefit of hindsight we understand easily enough that some prophecies referred to His First and some to His Second Coming.

Whilst on earth Jesus Christ personally made many of the most important prophecies of all, concerning what was still very much in the future and beyond the end of the current Jewish dispersion. We shall quote Luke 21:24 in our next chapter to substantiate this. It is therefore arrogance beyond belief that some should claim that all Old Testament prophecy was fulfilled in the birth, life, death and resurrection of Jesus Christ 2,000 years ago and that there are no further specific prophecies to be fulfilled on earth, particularly concerning the nation Israel.

For those who want to explore end-time prophecy in greater detail, I strongly recommend *"Outlines in Bible Prophecy"* by JW de Silva. It is a large ring-bound volume, with numerous tables, charts and illustrations. My own *'The Minor Prophets and the End Times'* and *'End Time Prophecy in the Gospels'* are more specific, as the titles indicate. All are recent publications by John Ritchie Limited.

CHAPTER TWO

Three Progressions
To The End Times

The term 'the End Times' is taken to refer to what follows the end of the Church Age; this involves not only momentous events leading up to the Lord's return in power and glory, but also the return itself and subsequent happenings on earth. In chapter 3 we will begin to examine the programme as we find it revealed in outline in Scripture. But it will save endless explanations if we first look at the contrasting ways in which what we might call three groups of actors relate to the end-time stage. These three groups are (a) Israel, (b) a sequence of Gentile empires first revealed in the book of Daniel and (c) the Christian Church. I will be brief and give only bare outlines. The Bible does not give any prophetic details of Church Age events following the 70 AD sack of Jerusalem, but it does tell us rather a lot of what will happen thereafter, sufficient for us to be able to judge that this age is rapidly drawing to a close and that the end-time scene is being set.

ISRAEL'S PROGRESSION TOWARDS THE END TIMES
About four thousand years ago God chose Abram, whose name He later changed to Abraham, to be the father of a nation into which His Son would in the fullness of time be born as the Messiah. *"And I will make of thee a great nation, and I will bless thee, and make thy name great; and thou shalt be a blessing. And I will bless them that bless thee, and curse him that curseth thee: and in thee shall all families of the earth be blessed"*

(Genesis 12:2-3). As we shall see later, this prophesied blessing is far from complete and carries us into the End Times.

Subsequently this great promise was narrowed down to Abraham's son, Isaac, and then to his grandson, Jacob, whom God renamed Israel. Jacob had twelve sons, each of whom became the progenitor of a tribe. Collectively they became known as the Children of Israel or Israelites; the term Jew did not appear until hundreds of years later, but remains in common usage today. Where God gives privilege, He also allocates responsibility. When the Israelites had become a nation, God set before them, through that great leader Moses, a list of potential blessings and curses, which may be found listed in Deuteronomy chapters 28 to 30. These make fascinating reading, as they explain everything that has happened to Israel down through the succeeding three and a half thousand years. In Acts chapter 7 Stephen was martyred for demonstrating vividly to his national leaders that it was their persistent disobedience to God and to His covenants which had led to their many disasters.

Eventually, following the death of King Solomon, the nation was divided into two. The smaller southern kingdom of Judah survived when the northern kingdom was deported to Assyria in 722 BC, never to return as a national group. By the end of the book of Esther, around 210 years later, Jews were scattered throughout the 127 provinces of the Persian Empire. Providentially this meant that at the time of Jesus' crucifixion, resurrection and ascension, there was a multitude of Jewish pilgrims in Jerusalem from all over the world for the annual feasts. Many were converted on the day of Pentecost and took the Christian Gospel back to their homelands. God had given the Children of Israel a special witnessing role, as confirmed by Isaiah even after the deportation of the northern kingdom: *"Ye are My witnesses, saith the LORD, and My servant whom I have chosen: that ye may know and believe Me, and understand that I am He: before Me there was no God formed, neither shall there be after Me"* (43:10). This 43rd chapter of Isaiah is very revealing, demonstrating Israel's key witnessing role in both the past and the future, even although at present others, namely the Church, have taken over this responsibility for nigh on two thousand years. About 125 years after the northern kingdom's deportation, Judah was taken captive to Babylon for seventy years. Many of Judah returned along with Benjamites, a lot of priestly Levites and a few stragglers from other tribes. Thereafter there were some spiritual revivals, but much apostasy.

There are a number of pairs of apparently incompatible spiritual truths, comprehensible only after taking the first simple step of faith. This is not brain-washing; it is divine wisdom graciously imparted. One such pair of truths is that, at His first coming, Jesus genuinely and sincerely presented Himself as Messiah to His people, but knew full well that He would be rejected. The comment in the opening chapter of John's Gospel is poignant, but reveals ultimate blessing available to all mankind: *"He was in the world, and the world was made by him, and the world knew him not. He came unto his own, and his own received him not. But as many as received him, to them gave he power to become the sons of God, even to them that believe on his name"* (John 1:10-12). We Gentiles are the beneficiaries of Israel's rejection.

There came a point during Jesus' earthly ministry when the religious leaders, who had been monitoring His preaching, and whose hardness of heart He had often rebuked, announced that, despite the fact that they conformed to Messianic prophecies, His miracles were Satanically empowered. (Matthew 12:14-24). It was only following this astonishing accusation that He limited His teaching of the crowds to parables, having reconfirmed the pronouncement of Isaiah 6:9-10: *"Therefore speak I to them in parables: because they seeing see not; and hearing they hear not, neither do they understand. And in them is fulfilled the prophecy of Esaias, which saith, By hearing ye shall hear, and shall not understand; and seeing ye shall see, and shall not perceive For this people's heart is waxed gross, and their ears are dull of hearing, and their eyes they have closed; lest at any time they should see with their eyes, and hear with their ears, and should understand with their heart, and should be converted, and I should heal them"* (Matthew 13:13-15). The stages of Jesus' ministry become much more comprehensible if we notice His progressive responses to these changes in national attitudes

When, on what we call Palm Sunday, Jesus presented Himself to His city, in vivid fulfilment of the promise of Zechariah 9:9, the crowds of pilgrims on the roadside welcomed Him. But the supposedly awaiting city spurned Him; a humble and lowly King did not conform to their aspirations. A spiritually undemanding military Messiah who would free the land from the Roman yoke would have been more to their liking. Weeping over the city, He cried: *"O Jerusalem, Jerusalem, thou that killest the prophets, and stonest them which are sent unto thee, how often would I have gathered thy children together, even as a hen gathereth her chickens under her wings, and ye would not! Behold, your house is left unto you desolate. For I say unto you, Ye shall not see me henceforth, till ye shall say, Blessed is he that cometh in the name of the Lord"* (Matthew 23:37-39). In a later chapter we will see how that *"Till ye say"* will at last be fulfilled. Note well: Jesus said *"until"* and not "unless". There are actually many Christians who ignore this vital point.

Less than forty years later the Romans sacked Jerusalem, as Jesus had foretold: *"And they shall fall by the edge of the sword, and shall be led away captive into all nations: and Jerusalem shall be trodden down of the Gentiles, until the times of the Gentiles be fulfilled"* (Lk 21:24). The Times of the Gentiles have yet to end; Jews still do not have undisputed ownership of their ancient capital city. This introduces us to the progress of both the Gentile empires and the Church towards end-time events.

PROGRESSION OF GENTILE EMPIRES TOWARDS THE END TIMES

On many occasions in both Old and New Testaments, Jesus is revealed as the King of David's line of the royal tribe of Judah (Genesis 49:10, Psalm 89:24-37, Revelation 22:16 etc). Following the start of the Babylonian exile, the prophet Ezekiel, himself an exile in Babylonia, proclaimed: *"Thus saith the Lord GOD; Remove the diadem, and take off the crown: this shall not be the same: exalt him that is low, and abase him that is high. I will overturn, overturn, overturn it: and it shall be no more, until he come whose right it is; and I will give it him"* (Ezek 21:26-27). One of the Minor Prophets wrote: *"For the children of Israel shall abide many days without a king, and without a prince, and without a sacrifice, and without an image, and without an ephod, and without teraphim. Afterward shall the children of Israel return, and seek the LORD their God, and David their king; and shall fear the LORD and his goodness in the latter days"* (Hosea 3:4-5).. What can be clearer?

The interval from the last King of David's line to the next one to be crowned, in other words Jesus Christ Himself, is therefore a very long one indeed; we are still within that long interval. Those *'many days'* of Hosea's prophecy have yet to expire, but expire they will. In the meantime God has ordained a succession of Gentile emperors to occupy this interval, which, as we have just seen, Jesus called the Times of the Gentiles.

Nebuchadnezzar was king or emperor of Babylon when Judah was taken captive and Jerusalem was sacked. Let us look at the salient points of Daniel chapter 2; the chapter is quite long, but makes exciting reading. The book of Daniel is sometimes described as the O.T. apocalypse. Incidentally 'apocalypse' means unveiling or revelation, not catastrophe; film makers have not noticed! This Babylonian king had what seemed a nightmare, but was in fact a God-given vision, which Daniel was privileged to interpret. Nebuchadnezzar had seen a great statue, with a head of gold, upper body of silver, lower body of bronze, legs of iron and compound feet of iron and incompatible ceramic clay. The entire structure was ultimately to be toppled and destroyed by a stone or rock which would fill the world.

Daniel told him that he, the Babylonian emperor, was the head of gold, that his empire would be succeeded by the silver Medo-Persian Empire, that the bronze Greek Empire would follow, to be replaced by an iron empire which was not actually named, because Rome was unknown in Babylon at the time. Even the Greek identity must have amazed Nebuchadnezzar, because Greece was then an insignificant nation state in another continent, apparently posing no threat either to Babylonia or Persia. Note that all these empires at the height of their power occupied the Holy Land. Empires in other parts of the world do not come into the picture.

Now this Roman Empire takes us up, not only to the time of Jesus first coming, but also to the sack of Jerusalem in 70 AD and well into the Church Age. The Church cannot, as has been suggested, be the stone kingdom, as it co-existed with the Roman Empire for several centuries and the fifth iron–

plus-clay kingdom has yet to materialise. Prophetic details of what happens in the Church Age are given neither in O.T. nor N.T. prophecy. We know from Daniel, Revelation and elsewhere that the fifth empire of ten kingdoms, headed by the person whom the Bible calls the Beast, will dominate the world scene after the Church Age, and that his empire will be an enigmatic mix of the Roman iron and unidentified ceramic clay. To what extent there has been continuity of empire during the intervening centuries is debatable, but we should be looking out already for a political entity, with traceable imperial Roman forebears, which is to reach its zenith in the future – perhaps the near future, one which will dominate the area around the Holy Land and could possibly cover the entire land area of all the previous empires.

THE CHURCH'S PROGRESSION TOWARDS THE END TIMES

In Isaiah 43 we saw that in the past the Jews were God's chief witnesses, and that in the future they will be again. But in the meantime witnessing is primarily the responsibility of the Christian Church; in fact we are called ambassadors: *"Now then, we are ambassadors for Christ, as though God were pleading through us: we implore you on Christ's behalf, be reconciled to God"* (II Corinthians 5:20 NKJV). What a privilege! What a responsibility! Of course Israel is still witnessing to God's faithfulness by default; she has long been suffering neither more nor less than the conditions graphically laid down, before her entry into the Promised Land. An old but very useful analogy is that of Israel having occupied the mainline in God's purposes until she was side-lined because of her failures. In the meantime the Church occupies the mainline and will do so until she is called home and Israel comes back on track. All of this was foreknown by God, who included it in His timetable for those who are prepared to take the trouble to look.

In the meantime we are in what we call the Church Age, when Israel's house is *left desolate*. It will remain desolate until then: *"'Simon has declared how God at the first visited the Gentiles to take out of them a people for His name. And with this the words of the prophets agree, just as it is written: "After this I will return And will rebuild the tabernacle of David, which has fallen down; I will rebuild its ruins, And I will set it up; so that the rest of mankind may seek the LORD, Even all the Gentiles who are called by My name, Says the LORD who does all these things."'"* (Acts 15:14-17 NKJV, quoting Amos 9:10-11). Simon is of course Simon Peter and *'at the first'* refers to the birth of the Church, which would have been about thirteen years old when James referred to Peter's quotation.

It is very clear that the Church, which had a start point, is also to have a finishing point; and that finishing point will be long before the end of the world, because further things have been foretold. David's tabernacle has to be rebuilt on the same planet as it formerly stood! There has to be a restoration of Israel one day, not a permanent replacement; God said so. Who dares disagree? Unfortunately many dare to; it's called Replacement Theology and is a dreadful distortion of God's faithfulness. I have dealt with it in my lengthy book, *'Apocalypse Facts and Fantasies'* (Twoedged Sword). By the 4th Century A.D. apostasy and false teaching were becoming prevalent, and apathy towards predictive prophecy was growing. The creeds of that time condensed into a few words a subject to which Scripture allots a vast amount of space. As a result, many Christians expect the world to end with Christ's return and expect the Church to remain active upon earth until that day. Also Anti-Semitism was growing. Of course Jews brought it upon themselves, and many do not exactly make themselves loveable; but that in no way exonerates anybody else. Hatred and persecution of Jews is abhorrent to God, and those who practise it incur

His wrath. *"He who touches you touches the apple of His eye"*, says the prophet Zechariah (2:8).

So how will the Church Age end and the End Times begin? Jesus on the night of His betrayal promised the Eleven after Judas Iscariot had left: *"In my Father's house are many mansions: if it were not so, I would have told you. I go to prepare a place for you. And if I go and prepare a place for you, I will come again, and receive you unto myself; that where I am, there ye may be also"* (John 14:2-3). The *fact* of the promise is clear, but the *how* of the promise Jesus left for the apostle Paul to explain, well into the early Church Age. 'Mansions' would be better rendered 'dwelling places' – sorry!

Each human being is a trinity - spirit, soul and body: *"And the very God of peace sanctify you wholly; and I pray God your whole spirit and soul and body be preserved blameless unto the coming of our Lord Jesus Christ"* (I Thessalonians 5:23). When Jesus rose from the dead it was bodily. *"But now is Christ risen from the dead, and become the firstfruits of them that slept"* (I Corinthians 15:20). There is an indication in Matthew 27:51-53 that a number of Old Testament saints rose with or shortly after Jesus and were also taken to Heaven as a symbolic first sheaf of a future great harvest. But most O.T. saints await a future resurrection – even great heroes like King David (Acts 2:29, 34). No Church believer has yet risen bodily. One day soon, we believe, the Church is to be united corporately to proceed to the place Jesus has gone to prepare; how soon we don't know. The Lord wants us to be ever prepared. The idea that Mary, Peter and other 'saints' are already resurrected in Heaven was absorbed from paganism, to keep happy those who had previously had on hand a whole assortment of heathen gods and goddesses. All New Testament believers were called saints, and some were not all that saintly! When a believer comes to the end of this earthly life, only the body actually dies. The souls and spirits are with the Lord, incomplete without the body, but nevertheless in a blessed and conscious state.

So how and when will the Church find itself complete in Heaven, both individually and corporately? The answer is to be found in I Thessalonians 4:13-18: *"But I would not have you to be ignorant, brethren, concerning them which are asleep, that ye sorrow not, even as others which have no hope. For if we believe that Jesus died and rose again, even so them also which sleep in Jesus will God bring with him. For this we say unto you by the word of the Lord, that we which are alive and remain unto the coming of the Lord shall not prevent them which are asleep. For the Lord himself shall descend from heaven with a shout, with the voice of the archangel, and with the trump of God: and the dead in Christ shall rise first: Then we which are alive and remain shall be caught up together with them in the clouds, to meet the Lord in the air: and so shall we ever be with the Lord. Wherefore comfort one another with these words."* The word 'prevent' in the A.V. should be rendered 'precede'. The Thessalonians had been worried that loved ones who had just died had missed out! The comfort was for them and every succeeding generation.

For the dead or 'sleeping' in Christ, this glorious future event will mean coming only as far as the clouds with Jesus to receive their glorious new bodies, like Jesus' own. For those still alive on earth, it will be their catching up to the clouds, to be transformed from the corruptible to incorruptible, to be for ever with our Lord. This will be the fulfilment of Jesus' promise in John 14:3 to come FOR us, that is those who believe, rather than TO us, after which we *will ever be with the Lord*. This event is usually referred to as the 'Rapture', from the Latin word for 'catch up'. People who believe the Bible may argue about the timing and even the most suitable name for the event, but not about the bare facts.

Paul told the church at Corinth about what would happen to believers' bodies at the Rapture: *"So also is the resurrection of the dead. It is sown in corruption; it is raised in incorruption: It is sown in dishonour; it is raised in glory: it is sown in weakness; it is raised in power: It is sown a natural body; it is raised a spiritual body. There is a natural body, and there is a spiritual body...... Behold, I shew you a mystery; We shall not all sleep, but we shall all be changed, In a moment, in the twinkling of an eye, at the last trump: for the trumpet shall sound, and the dead shall be raised incorruptible, and we shall be changed. For this corruptible must put on incorruption, and this mortal must put on immortality"* (I Corinthians 15:42-44, 51-53).

What happens in Heaven once we get there we can leave until subsequent chapters. Suffice it to say here and now that no preconditions are laid down for the Rapture; every Christian should be ready and eager. But signs of the times certainly make it seem more likely than ever before, as we see looming large on the horizon the quite dramatic build-up to conditions which are to prevail, and to events which are to happen and to personalities who are to appear *after* the Rapture, when the End Times proper begin. Note well that, *"we shall not all sleep"* promise. Never dying is a real possibility, ever more likely as the signs of the times multiply.

CHAPTER THREE

The Horsemen Of The Apocalypse

HOW THE END TIMES BEGIN

In Chapter 2 we saw that the End Times are going to begin with all saints of the Church Age safely called home and in Heaven. But the rest of Israel and the Gentile nations will remain upon earth. God is going to have a showdown with humankind, which is becoming ever more cruel, warlike and ungodly. He had such a showdown before: *"And the LORD said, 'My Spirit shall not strive with man forever, for he is indeed flesh; yet his days shall be one hundred and twenty years.'..... Then the LORD saw that the wickedness of man was great in the earth, and that every intent of the thoughts of his heart was only evil continually. And the LORD was sorry that He had made man on the earth, and He was grieved in His heart. So the LORD said, 'I will destroy man whom I have created from the face of the earth, both man and beast, creeping thing and birds of the air, for I am sorry that I have made them.'"* (Genesis 6:3,5,6,7 NKJV). Three chapters further on we find that God said that He would never send another world-wide flood, but did not revoke the right to judge.

However we will also find that during this coming dreadful time mercy will be shown. There will be ample provision for people to repent and become right with their Creator – unprecedented opportunities which we shall consider later. But now is very much the best time to be right with God. In II Thessalonians 2:10-12 there is a warning that those who consciously put off accepting Jesus Christ as Saviour now will be unable to repent later; they will be deceived.

We may speculate how the Rapture of the saints will be explained by world authorities; there has been some reasonable and some wild guesswork, but, as we are not told, it seems pointless to discuss possibilities here. However we can be certain that there is bound to be a huge impact as hundreds of millions suddenly disappear. Moreover countries which have had large influential Christian populations are likely to change political alignment in a fluid international situation. Revelation 7:9 tells us of a vast number of converts from every nation, tribe, people and language. Bibles are likely to be treasured as never before; eventually they may become banned. But those who read them will be in no doubt about the identity of the Beast, the ruler of a great empire which some think will be a world-wide dominion, although I am among those who think it will be more limited. Having read Jesus' Olivet Discourse, they will know to watch out for blasphemous events centred at Jerusalem, and those who live in and around that city will be preparing to flee at a moment's notice.

WORSE AND WORSE!
This Tribulation Period of the End Times is going to be progressive in intensity. We find the outline programme revealed in two books – Daniel and Revelation. The Church Age is skipped over completely in Daniel. Those who may wish later to note where this long and important interval fits will find it in Daniel 2 between verses 40 and 41, in 7 between vv 23 and 24, in 8 between vv 22 and 23, in 9 between vv 26 and 27 and in 11 between vv 35 and 36, but one needs a good commentary. The Daniel prophecies are confirmed by Jesus Himself in His Olivet Discourse on the End Times which He gave His disciples only two days before His arrest and three

days before His crucifixion, and which is covered in Matthew 24 and 25, Mark 13 and Luke 21. It must surely be extremely important. In the section entitled 'Gabriel's Earlier Announcement' later in this chapter, we will see that the Tribulation Period is to last little more than seven years. Many other books of the Bible, especially the Major and Minor Prophets, contribute to our knowledge of this time. The N.T. epistles rarely touch on it, because the Church will not be on earth then.

Some end-time prophecies, such as the afore-mentioned Olivet Discourse, are plainly stated and concern what is to happen on earth. Obviously one has to make allowance for the fact that all Bible prophecy has had to make some sense during the intervening centuries. Had He chosen to, God could easily have described inter-continental ballistic missiles and implant chips in a way that only 21st Century readers would understand; but He chose not to. Revelation from chapter 4 relates what the Apostle John saw when caught up to Heaven in the Spirit (4:1). It was utterly new to him, he described his visions as they were presented to him; sometimes he gave explanations with the help of an interpreting angel. He was in fact amazingly successful, because, allowing for some imponderables, there is much which we, with 21st Century knowledge, can intelligently surmise from his account, whilst other things will make sense to believers on earth only when they occur. For many centuries some of the events prophesied in the middle portion of the Book of Revelation must have appeared random and unconnected; only a divinely inspired prophet could have foretold future horrors where modern scientists can perceive the 'cause and effect factor' – the correlation between apparently disparate phenomena. How the absence of the Mark of the Beast (Revelation 13:16-17) in a hand or forehead could prevent people from buying or selling was much less comprehensible when I first read it as a teenager around 1949 than it is now in the computer age, when scanners are part of everyday life. Those in years gone by who believed God's word simply accepted it and trusted Him. God is nobody's debtor; trusting Him now will guarantee eternal dividends.

Jesus called the first half of this coming Tribulation Period *'The Beginning of Sorrows'* (Matthew 24:8) and the second half *'Great Tribulation'* (Matthew 24:21) – described as *'THE Great Tribulation'* in Revelation 7:14. In this chapter we will concentrate on the Beginning of Sorrows. As we shall see later in this chapter, Daniel 9:27 tells us of the seven year duration of the Tribulation Period, whilst Daniel 12:7, Revelation 12:6, 12:14 and 13:5 refer to its two equal divisions as 'three and a half years', '42 months', 'half a week', '1260 days', 'times, time and half a time', lest any try to deny or fiddle with the figures! Jesus Himself referred to what was to happen at the mid-point as we saw in our previous chapter, and two Gospel writers instructed readers to understand (Matthew 24:15, Mark 13:14).

THE RIGHTEOUS JUDGE

Paul told the Athenians: *"And the times of this ignorance God winked at; but now commandeth all men everywhere to repent: Because he hath appointed a day, in the which he will judge the world in righteousness by that man whom he hath ordained; whereof he hath given assurance unto all men, in that he hath raised him from the dead"* (Acts 17:30-31). The word translated here as 'day' can be used for 'time' or 'occasion'. Jesus made it very clear that He had not come to judge at His First Coming (John 12:47), but that He nevertheless was His Father's appointed Judge: *"So hath he given to the Son to have life in himself: And hath given him authority to execute judgment also, because he is the Son of man"* (John 5:27). He is uniquely qualified: *"He... was in all points tempted like as we are, yet without sin Hebrews"*

(4:15), *"And they sung a new song, saying, Thou art worthy to take the book, and to open the seals thereof: for thou wast slain, and hast redeemed us to God by thy blood out of every kindred, and tongue, and people, and nation"* (Revelation 5:9). At His Second Coming Christ will accomplish what, in order to complete His work of salvation, He chose not to do at His First.

Thus it is the risen and glorified Lord Jesus Christ Himself who is to set in motion the chain of events which are to comprise the Tribulation Period. The chapter break between Revelation 4 and 5 is unfortunate, because it is a single vision. Chapter 1 of Revelation introduces this awesome book. John was instructed by the risen Lord Himself: *"And when I saw him, I fell at his feet as dead. And he laid his right hand upon me, saying unto me, Fear not; I am the first and the last: I am he that liveth, and was dead; and, behold, I am alive for evermore, Amen; and have the keys of hell and of death. Write the things which thou hast seen, and the things which are, and the things which shall be hereafter"* (Revelation 1:17-19). The next two chapters tell us something about *"the things which are"*, the contemporary church situation at the end of the 1st Century AD when John recorded His vision. Here are powerful and salutary messages for the entire Church Age. Have you compared your congregation, if you have one, with these seven little churches in Asia Minor? In one of them, the Laodicean church, Jesus was actually locked out and seeking entrance (Revelation 3:20); there are churches like that today, which are blissfully unaware that their Lord is no longer in their midst.

In Revelation chapters 4 and 5, the aged Apostle John, who has been called to Heaven to see what is to happen *hereafter*, sees not only mighty angelic beings, but also the raptured Church, with saints casting down their newly awarded crowns, given to those who have served faithfully whilst on earth (see II Timothy 4:8, James 1:12 and 1 Peter 5:4 etc). A seven sealed scroll appears, containing consecutive authorisations to release onto the earth below events and personages of the Tribulation Period, as one by one the seals are broken. Only Jesus Christ, who is introduced as a Lion but appears as a Lamb, is found worthy: *"And one of the elders saith unto me, Weep not: behold, the Lion of the tribe of Juda, the Root of David, hath prevailed to open the book, and to loose the seven seals thereof. And I beheld, and, lo, in the midst of the throne and of the four beasts, and in the midst of the elders, stood a Lamb as it had been slain"* (Revelation 5:5-6). The book of Revelation alternates between Heaven and earth; what John saw in Heaven he had to describe as best he could, but when happenings on earth are described, we should take them at face value as far as possible.

FOUR HORSEMEN

The first four seals reveal consecutively the Horsemen of the Apocalypse; that is how they were presented to John. *"And I saw when the Lamb opened one of the seven seals, and I heard one of the four living creatures saying, as a voice of thunder, Come and see. And I saw: and behold, a white horse, and he that sat upon it having a bow; and a crown was given to him, and he went forth conquering and that he might conquer. And when it opened the second seal, I heard the second living creature saying, Come and see. And another, a red horse, went forth; and to him that sat upon it, to him it was given to take peace from the earth, and that they should slay one another; and there was given to him a great sword. And when it opened the third seal, I heard the third living creature saying, Come and see. And I saw: and behold, a black horse, and he that sat upon it having a balance in his hand. And I heard as a voice in the midst of the four living creatures saying, A choenix of wheat for a denarius, and three choenixes of barley for a denarius: and do not injure the oil and the wine. And when it opened the fourth seal, I heard the voice of the fourth living creature saying,*

a measure of wheat for a penny
Three measures of barley for a penny

43

Come and see. And I saw: and behold, a pale horse, and he that sat upon it, his name was Death, and hades followed with him; and authority was given to him over the fourth of the earth to slay with sword, and with hunger, and with death, and by the beasts of the earth" (Revelation 6:1-8 JND). A choenix is a day's ration and a denarius a day's pay.

The picture is remarkably clear; perhaps the only ambiguous statement is that regarding the measures of barley. Effectively it is declaring that a measure of the most staple diet grain will cost a full day's wage, whilst luxury items will be spared for those who can afford them. That sort of thing happens in any corrupt society and especially in wartime.

Some have assumed that the first rider depicts Christ Himself; that could not be further from the truth. There are a number of contrasts between this person and the other Rider on the white horse whom we will encounter in Revelation 19 – that is indeed Jesus Christ. This is a representation of the false or 'Anti-Christ', later described as the First Beast, with no arrow to his bow, who is to appear on the world stage, and initially by intrigue and manipulation, rather than military might, take control in a planet desperate for strong leadership. Many of the worst despots in human history have started their careers as apparently benevolent dictators. Where they make no demands for holiness and godliness, they are welcomed by the masses. This will be Satan's man, and even Satan is capable of appearing as an angel of light (II Corinthians 11:14). It is reasonable to assume that, since the earliest days of the Church Age, Satan has always had his man standing by to step into this role, a new one being groomed whenever one has died. God is in due course going to sanction the appearance of this dynamic ruler in order to compel all individuals to make a decision 'for or against' their rightful King. We have much more to say about this portentous personage later, but let us move on to the second horse.

In the days leading up to the Rapture there will be wars a-plenty, but following the Rapture there will be global power struggles, too complex for us to be able to identify all the contending power blocs; there is no need for us to consider the options in this little book. Their conflicts are represented by the red horse and rider. Only the Beast's great end-time empire, the final of the series of five which we saw in the previous chapter, is central to our prophetic study. Wherever there is war, poverty and starvation, disease and death are among the consequences. This is the black horse with his ominous rider bearing scales. The final horse is a ghastly pale greenish colour, bringing ever increasing death in a variety of ways. In October 2011 the world's population reached seven billion; by the opening of the seventh seal it will be greatly depleted.

Now many people have tried hard to fit the seven seals, and subsequent seven trumpets and seven bowls of wrath of the book of Revelation into a precise time scale; personally I feel that some have been rather too ingenious. If we try to put the series of seals, trumpets and bowls end-to-end we face all sorts of problems. In fact all three series take us up to Christ's Coming in Power – compare Revelation 6:12-17 or 11:15-18 or 16:17-21. The three series may thus be said to be coterminous – starting sequentially but reaching the same climax. Events and personages revealed by seals, trumpets and bowls do not necessarily disappear with the next in the sequence but may remain to the end. Thus we may reasonably say that the opening of the first four horsemen seals sets the scene for the Beginning of Sorrows – that which is to start very soon after the Rapture, but which will continue to apply throughout the entire Tribulation Period.

THE BEGINNING OF SORROWS

The Beginning of Sorrows is summarised by Jesus in Matthew 24:3-14. I recommend reading the whole passage, but here are a few short extracts: *"And as he sat upon the mount of Olives, the disciples came unto him privately, saying, Tell us, when shall these things be? and what shall be the sign of thy coming, and of the end of the world?"* (v 3). The disciples did not yet realise that they were enquiring about two separate events. *"And ye shall hear of wars and rumours of wars: see that ye be not troubled: for all these things must come to pass, but the end is not yet. For nation shall rise against nation, and kingdom against kingdom: and there shall be famines, and pestilences, and earthquakes, in divers places. All these are the beginning of sorrows"* (vv 6-8). This is what the four 'horsemen' seals revealed.

"And many false prophets shall rise, and shall deceive many. And because iniquity shall abound, the love of many shall wax cold. But he that shall endure unto the end, the same shall be saved. And this gospel of the kingdom shall be preached in all the world for a witness unto all nations; and then shall the end come" (vv 11-14). All these things have, of course happened before; they will simply be more intense and concentrated. Thereafter we find ourselves at the start of the Great Tribulation, to be covered in the next chapter, when truly catastrophic and unprecedented events are to take place. The 'end' here is the end of the Tribulation period, and being 'saved' refers to the coming rescue of believers. People are saved from their sins the moment they accept Jesus Christ as personal Saviour, rather than following a life time's perseverance.

GOD'S TRIBULATION WITNESSES

I recall being told in science classes at school that nature hates a vacuum. Often people talk about impersonal 'nature' or 'Mother Nature', rather than admit to the God who they know must be there because of the evidence of their own eyes, but refuse to acknowledge. God is not going to allow for an evangelisation vacuum or complete absence of witnesses after the Rapture of the Church. Once the seals have been enumerated, we are introduced to God's main Tribulation Period witnesses: *"Hurt not the earth, neither the sea, nor the trees, till we have sealed the servants of our God in their foreheads. And I heard the number of them which were sealed: and there were sealed an hundred and forty and four thousand of all the tribes of the children of Israel"* (Revelation 7:3-4). Now we are not specifically told that these are evangelists, but they are evidently sealed for some purpose, and immediately after their tribes are declared, we read: *"After these things I looked, and behold, a great multitude which no one could number, of all nations, tribes, peoples, and tongues, standing before the throne and before the Lamb, clothed with white robes, with palm branches in their hands, and crying out with a loud voice, saying, "Salvation belongs to our God who sits on the throne, and to the Lamb!"* (Revelation 7:9:10). These are identified not as Church Age saints but as Tribulation saints. *"Then one of the elders answered, saying to me, 'Who are these arrayed in white robes, and where did they come from?' And I said to him, 'Sir, you know.' So he said to me, 'These are the ones who come out of the great tribulation, and washed their robes and made them white in the blood of the Lamb'."* (Revelation 7:13-14 NKJV).

Even today there are tens of thousands of Orthodox Jews who are steeped in the O.T. Scriptures, just as Paul was nearly two thousand years ago. Like Paul, they were zealous for God but blind to the identity of their Messiah until God's Holy Spirit came upon them; *"And Ananias went his way, and entered into the house; and putting his hands on him said, Brother Saul, the Lord, even Jesus, that appeared unto thee in the way as thou camest, hath sent me, that thou mightest receive thy sight, and be filled with the Holy Ghost….. And straightway he preached Christ in the synagogues, that he is the Son of God".* (Acts 9:17-

18, 20). Just as long ago Saul of Tarsus became the Apostle Paul in an instant, so, probably very soon after the Rapture, God will seal His witnesses – He is going to need them to preach the Gospel of the Kingdom throughout the world (Matthew 24:14)

GABRIEL'S EARLIER ANNOUNCEMENT

What some students of Bible prophecy do not seem to notice is that a seven year period immediately prior to Christ's return in power has been declared to be specifically for the Jews – or Daniel's people. Some want to give only half that time to the Jews, and some none! Most people know that it was the mighty angel Gabriel who made the incredibly important announcement of the Saviour's birth. He is only one of two angels actually named in Scripture, the other being the Archangel Michael (Daniel 12:1, Jude 1:9). It is Gabriel (Daniel 9:21) who is entrusted to reveal the equal lengths of the two parts of the Tribulation Period, in a vision given to the elderly prophet, Daniel. This is a passage proscribed by some Orthodox rabbis, because its truths are so hateful to them. I will be as brief as possible; I have dealt with the passage in greater detail in other books.

It is very helpful to understand this graciously revealed end-time timetable, and I recommend that the whole of Daniel 9 be read in a non-paraphrased version of the Bible.: *"(v 24) Seventy weeks are apportioned out upon thy people and upon thy holy city, to close the transgression, and to make an end of sins, and to make expiation for iniquity, and to bring in the righteousness of the ages, and to seal the vision and prophet, and to anoint the holy of holies. (v 25) Know therefore and understand: From the going forth of the word to restore and to build Jerusalem unto Messiah, the Prince, are seven weeks, and sixty-two weeks. The street and the moat shall be built again, even in troublous times. (v 26) And after the sixty-two weeks shall Messiah be cut off, and shall have nothing; and the people of the prince that shall come shall destroy the city and the sanctuary; and the end thereof shall be with an overflow, and unto the end, war, — the desolations determined. (v 27) And he shall confirm a covenant with the many for one week; and in the midst of the week he shall cause the sacrifice and the oblation to cease, and because of the protection of abominations there shall be a desolator, even until that the consumption and what is determined shall be poured out upon the desolate.*" (Daniel 9:24-27 JND).

The people from which the end-time prince, who is identified elsewhere as the Beast, is to come are those who were to destroy the temple and its sanctuary, in other words the Romans in 70 AD. This is one reason why we talk of an end-time Revived Roman Empire, the other reason being the continuity of the iron from the fulfilled legs to the future feet of the image of Daniel chapter 2, which describes the Times of the Gentiles, which, though not revealed to Daniel, includes the entire Church Age. We should not be over-hasty in defining the exact constitution of this Revived Roman Empire; the current volatility of both the European Union and the Mediterranean Islamic states is something which the Beast may be the first to bring to order - for his own ends of course. Anybody who can achieve that will be hailed as a world-class leader.

The word translated 'week' can mean any heptad or group of seven. 490 lunar (360 day) years or 70 septennia were said to be allocated to (literally set aside for) Daniel's people, starting with a precisely identified day in 445 BC. This is about Jews, not the Gentile Church. We may forget here about the first division after 49 years, though it was very important at the time of rebuilding the defences of Jerusalem to confirm to people that God's promises were sure and being kept on schedule. We are thus left with two groups of 69 sevens or

483 elapsed years and 7 future years. The 483 elapsed years take us to what we call the first Palm Sunday, when Jesus as Messiah the Prince entered His city to be *"cut off"*. As we saw in our previous chapter, God transferred His witnessing thereafter to the Church until the end of the Church Age. Seven years are thus left in abeyance for Daniel's people until after the Rapture of the Church, as other references to this period confirm. I am sorry if this sounds complicated, but it is really very wonderful and is worth taking time to understand. Written simply, it amounts to:

$$7 + 62 + 1 = 70 \text{ groups of seven years}$$
$$\text{or } 49 + 434 + 7 = 490 \text{ years}$$

As soon as possible after the Rapture, the false prince, Antichrist or Beast is going either to negotiate or impose a seven year covenant with Israel. We may ask why he should do this if Satan hates Israel so much. Let us leave the answer until the next chapter. We do know from this chapter of Daniel and from II Thessalonians 2:4 and Revelation 11:1-2 that there must be such a future rebuilt Temple, with sacrifices and offerings resumed after many centuries, and that after three and a half years the Beast will break his covenant and stop these ordinances (Daniel 9:27).

AN ABORTIVE INVASION

Many commentators think that the invasion described in Ezekiel 38 and 39 is likely to occur during the Beginning of Sorrows, partly because it is very different in national identities and in outcome from the later wars of the Great Tribulation, and partly because the invader declares: *"And thou shalt say, I will go up to the land of unwalled villages; I will go to them that are at rest, that dwell safely, all of them dwelling without walls, and having neither bars nor gates"* (Ezekiel 38:11). Certainly history records no such invasion in the past. Verse

38:8 describes it as being in the distant future. Any militarily undefended Israel before the Rapture, and indeed before the seven year treaty with the coming emperor, seems highly improbable.

Oddly enough the identity of the *"Gog of the land of Magog"*, the prime mover in this invasion, is more doubtful than his allies. During the 19th Century Gog was thought to be due to arise from within the Ottoman Empire, but opinions switched to Anti-Semitic imperial Russia and then to the atheistic Soviet Union. Verse 38:15 says that Gog will be from the far North, and Moscow is almost due north of Jerusalem and very distant, and certainly Russia is currently Iran's most loyal ally. However there are instances in the O.T. where eastern nations approaching Israel via the usual Fertile Crescent route are said to be from the north, the direction of their crossing the national border. As far back as the 4th Century B.C., rabbis identified Gog as coming from the area of Afghanistan and Pakistan. Meschech and Tubal have sometimes been associated with Moscow and Tobolsk, but that is very tentative. All the allied nations described have long been Islamic, and one wonders how and why any Islamic jihad should be led by non-Muslims. *"Thus saith the Lord GOD; Behold, I am against thee, O Gog, the chief prince of Meschech and Tubal. And I will turn thee back, and put hooks into thy jaws, and I will bring thee forth, and all thine army, horses and horsemen, all of them clothed with all sorts of armour, even a great company with bucklers and shields, all of them handling swords: Persia, Ethiopia, and Libya with them; all of them with shield and helmet, Gomer, and all his bands; the house of Togarmah of the north quarters, and all his bands: and many people with thee"* (Ezekiel 38:3-6). Persia is of course Iran; Ethiopia refers more to the Sudan than the former Abyssinia, and Libya is simply Libya; Togarmah and Gomer are commonly identified with Turkey, though there are some doubts.

Ezekiel chapters 38 and 39 should be read in full. What is heavily emphasised is God's fury with these invaders and that the fact that Israel's victory is to be completely miraculous: *Therefore, son of man, prophesy and say unto Gog, Thus saith the Lord GOD; In that day when my people of Israel dwelleth safely, shalt thou not know it?...And thou shalt come up against my people of Israel, as a cloud to cover the land; it shall be in the latter days, and I will bring thee against my land, that the heathen may know me, when I shall be sanctified in thee, O Gog, before their eyes... And it shall come to pass at the same time when Gog shall come against the land of Israel, saith the Lord GOD, that my fury shall come up in my face. For in my jealousy and in the fire of my wrath have I spoken, Surely in that day there shall be a great shaking in the land of Israel;...And I will call for a sword against him throughout all my mountains, saith the Lord GOD: every man's sword shall be against his brother. And I will plead against him with pestilence and with blood; and I will rain upon him, and upon his bands, and upon the many people that are with him, an overflowing rain, and great hailstones, fire, and brimstone. Thus will I magnify myself, and sanctify myself; and I will be known in the eyes of many nations, and they shall know that I am the LORD* (Ezekiel 38:14,16, 18, 19, 21-23).

I have been at prayer meetings in 2011 when sincere believers have thanked God for the so-called Arab Spring and the overthrowing of oppressive dictatorship, and have optimistically prayed for democracy. I am not being cynical in thinking that they are naive; but I do feel that they neglect the signs of the times. Christian minorities in Islamic lands are in fact more, rather than less, vulnerable than before these revolutions, and the uncompromising Muslim Brotherhood is inciting even greater hatred of Israel. Coptic Christians in Egypt have suffered much greater persecution since President Mubarek was overthrown. There is going to be a great end-time invasion of Israel. God is going to demonstrate

His power in a truly spectacularly miraculous end-time victory, which will eclipse totally the Six Day War and Yom Kippur War victories in decisiveness. Not only will massive earthquakes devastate the invaders, but these armies will be compelled by God to destroy each other, as happened in the days of Gideon (Judges 7:22). Could this be Shia and Sunni annihilating each other? Recent tendencies suggest such a possibility, but we do not know. All will be completely destroyed, as irrefutable evidence of the power of God (38:23).; this is clearer in modern translations. This will be part of the divinely provided evidence which will help people to make personal decisions which will have an eternal impact.

Should there be a prior invasion of Israel by Arab neighbours in the meantime, which many Orthodox Jews expect in fulfilment of Ezekiel's prophecy, it seems highly improbable that it will be against a defenceless Israel. God has given unique talents to Jews down through the centuries, which have contributed to an amazing defensive capability. It is astonishing that there is so little recognition in so-called Christian nations that this is God-given. There is no doubt that God has three times enabled the underdog to achieve notable victories over superior forces since the nation was reborn in 1948, but the expertise of Israeli generals, the technical superiority of Israeli arms, the dedication of Israel's forces and the brilliance of their military intelligence have always played some part and been widely recognised. I write as a former Army officer with intelligence experience. In the Ezekiel invasion only Israel's God and ours will have the credit and the glory. Unless it fulfils that prophecy in full, we will know that a further invasion must take place. The leaders of the Islamic Republic of Iran, who pay more attention to Shi-ite prophecy than any modern 'Christian' nation does to Bible prophecy, make no secret of the fact that they believe that current Middle East revolutions point to the near arrival of the 12th Imam who they believe will destroy Israel.

MIRACLE WORKING WITNESSES

We have already seen from Daniel 9:27 that the Jerusalem temple will be rebuilt and will be permitted to function during the Beginning of Sorrows, as part of the seven year covenant with the fifth emperor, who is the Beast. But there will be restrictions, according to Revelation 11:1-:2: *"And there was given me a reed like unto a rod: and the angel stood, saying, Rise, and measure the temple of God, and the altar, and them that worship therein. But the court which is without the temple leave out, and measure it not; for it is given unto the Gentiles: and the holy city shall they tread under foot forty and two months"*. This will be the first half of the three and a half years – prophetic years as we have seen are always 360 day lunar years.

We have already seen something of the 144,000 witnesses; but God will provide two more mightily empowered special witnesses, who will in defiance of the godless emperor preach impending doom to those who do not repent and turn back to God. Evidently they will restrain the Beast from defiling the Temple itself until God permits this to happen at the midpoint of the covenant: *"And I will give power unto my two witnesses, and they shall prophesy a thousand two hundred and threescore days, clothed in sackcloth"* (Revelation 11:3). Like Elijah and Elisha of old they will be given divine protection and will be enabled to perform judgmental miracles: *"And if any man will hurt them, fire proceedeth out of their mouth, and devoureth their enemies: and if any man will hurt them, he must in this manner be killed. These have power to shut heaven, that it rain not in the days of their prophecy: and have power over waters to turn them to blood, and to smite the earth with all plagues, as often as they will"* (Revelation 11:5-6). This kind of miracle is further proof that the Church Age will be over; no Christian apostle has ever had such a mission. These two will not be on earth to preach the Gospel so much as to warn of the consequences of failure to repent; they will demonstrate that their authority comes from above, with what insurance companies would describe as 'acts of God'.

Commenting on the 2010 Icelandic volcano, which I have seen, a leading vulcanologist said that the massive disruption caused by what was far from Iceland's most powerful volcano "drove home how vulnerable modern society is to whims of nature". These witnesses will make it clear that what is happening and about to happen will be no mere 'whims of nature'; they will be dire warnings from their Creator which men and women will ignore at the peril of their eternal souls. God is amazingly merciful, but sets His own cut-off points for those who flout that mercy.

Clearly many will repent, confirming that one is the prophesied Elijah, who never died, returning from Heaven: *"Behold, I will send you Elijah the prophet before the coming of the great and dreadful day of the LORD: And he shall turn the heart of the fathers to the children, and the heart of the children to their fathers, lest I come and smite the earth with a curse"* (Malachi 4:5-6). John the Baptist might have fulfilled this role had he not been rejected (Matthew 11:13 and Mark 9:13). This curse withdrawn implies total destruction averted, in accordance with Jesus' words: *"And except those days should be shortened, there should no flesh be saved: but for the elect's sake those days shall be shortened"* (Matthew 24:22). The other witness may be Enoch, who never died, but was taken alive to Heaven like Elijah (Genesis 5:24 and II Kings 2:11).

In the subsequent verses we find that at the mid-point the Beast will be permitted to slay them: *"And when they shall have finished their testimony, the beast that ascendeth out of the bottomless pit shall make war against them, and shall overcome them, and kill them"* (Revelation 11:7), and that there will be world-wide celebration until God suddenly raises them from the dead and they ascend visibly to Heaven. At this point there will be a huge earthquake – God's vindication of His servants (see Revelation 11:8-13). This Beast from the pit will probably prove to be Satan himself; the other two Beasts who comprise the trinity of evil are from elsewhere. This will be the start of the Great Tribulation.

CHAPTER FOUR

The Brink Of Disaster

IN PERSPECTIVE

We are about to consider the blackest period in earth's history. But let us keep it in perspective; it will be a mercifully short period. The first four verses of Isaiah chapter 61 have sometimes been aptly described as the Messianic Mission Statement – a summary of what Jesus Christ became Man to accomplish. Let's briefly forget the verse divisions, which were added long ago for ease of reference, and look at this passage as a three stage progression which began to be fulfilled at the outset of His ministry, but is still far from completion:-

a) The Spirit of the Lord GOD is upon me; because the LORD hath anointed me to preach good tidings unto the meek; he hath sent me to bind up the brokenhearted, to proclaim liberty to the captives, and the opening of the prison to them that are bound; to proclaim the acceptable year of the LORD, and
b) The day of vengeance of our God;
c) To comfort all that mourn; to appoint unto them that mourn in Zion, to give unto them beauty for ashes, the oil of joy for mourning, the garment of praise for the spirit of heaviness; that they might be called trees of righteousness, the planting of the LORD, that he might be glorified. And they shall build the old wastes, they shall raise up the former desolations, and they shall repair the waste cities, the desolations of many generations.

Early in His ministry, Jesus in His own synagogue (local place of worship) read from this Isaiah scroll as far as *"the acceptable day of the Lord"*. But note what happened next: *"And he closed the book, and he gave it again to the minister, and sat down. And the eyes of all them that were in the synagogue were fastened on him. And he began to say unto them, This day is this scripture fulfilled in your ears"* (Lk 4:20-21). His sudden closure of the scroll is significant enough to be recorded for all generations. Part a) of the prophecy started then and there and continues to this very day. Part b) still lies ahead, and part c) even further ahead in this simple sequence. Two chapters later Isaiah indicates the comparative length of the restoration: *"For the **day** of vengeance is in mine heart, and the **year** of my redeemed is come"* (Isa 63:4). We therefore have in this Messianic Mission Statement God's declared plan for the earth and its inhabitants from Jesus' First Coming to the end of this planet, namely a) a long Church Age, b) a short Tribulation Period, c) a long Millennium.

THE ULTIMATE BLASPHEMY

In the previous chapter we asked why, if Satan hates Israel, should the Beast conclude a covenant which involves a rebuilt Jerusalem Temple with ancient sacrifices resumed. The answer is that Satan craves the ultimate blasphemy of placing on the Mercy Seat, the holiest place in the Temple, his own substitute messiah, who will publicly acknowledge his diabolical overlord: *"Let no man deceive you by any means: for that day shall not come, except there come a falling away first, and that man of sin be revealed, the son of perdition; Who opposeth and exalteth himself above all that is called God, or that is worshipped; so that he as God sitteth in the temple of God, shewing himself that he is God"* (II Thessalonians 2:3-4). He cannot do that unless there is a Jewish temple in Jerusalem. That will first have to be rebuilt. For Satan it will be a small price to pay. Already virtually all the pieces and equipment are stored, awaiting the signal to build. Currently the presence of two Islamic mosques on the Temple Mount is as big an obstacle as anybody could imagine. There are a number of suggestions as to how these buildings could be removed, assuming that they will be removed, including a rogue Syrian or Iranian rocket during some prior conflict! That is hardly far-fetched. There is actually space between them for the Temple, although such an arrangement seems highly unlikely. Will the coming war of Ezekiel 38 and 39 covered in our previous chapter, neutralise Islamic opposition? We must wait and see.

A DRAGON PURSUES A WOMAN
Now understandably most readers are likely to be concerned about the global situation rather than with what is happening in Israel. But, just as something which happened in Jerusalem two thousand years ago changed the world, so what is to happen there in the future will signal the world-wide Great Tribulation. Now Heaven is not bound by time the way we are on earth, and centuries may apparently be skipped over lightly. The woman of Revelation 12 is Israel, not Mary, as a brief look at Joseph's dream in Genesis 37:9 and its context confirms, as does the Olivet Discourse. Sculptors and artists have had a field day with a mistaken identity! Israel brought forth a Messiah, who, in what is still the future, will rule the nations with a rod of iron (Psalm 2:9, Revelation 19:15). He was at His ascension caught up to Heaven. In the following passage we see the woman pursued by a Dragon, of whom we will see more soon, who hates her. Suddenly we find ourselves at the mid-point of the Tribulation Period, where a desert refuge has been prepared for her. *"And there appeared a great wonder in heaven; a woman clothed with the sun, and the moon under her feet, and upon her head a crown of twelve stars: And she being with child cried, travailing in birth, and pained to be delivered. And there appeared another wonder in heaven; and*

behold a great red dragon, having seven heads and ten horns, and seven crowns upon his heads. And his tail drew the third part of the stars of heaven, and did cast them to the earth: and the dragon stood before the woman which was ready to be delivered, for to devour her child as soon as it was born. And she brought forth a man child, who was to rule all nations with a rod of iron: and her child was caught up unto God, and to his throne. And the woman fled into the wilderness, where she hath a place prepared of God, that they should feed her there a thousand two hundred and threescore days" (Revelation 12:1-6).

We recognise the three-and-a-half year duration of the refuge from Daniel 9:27. Jesus warned: *"When ye therefore shall see the abomination of desolation, spoken of by Daniel the prophet, stand in the holy place, (whoso readeth, let him understand:) Then let them which be in Judaea flee into the mountains"* (Matthew 24:15-16). Mark 13:14-15 gives the same warning.

THE FINAL HOLOCAUST
The many Jews, wherever they are, who are not in a position to flee to the desert sanctuary, are to undergo a final Holocaust – the word means 'burnt offering'. God has permitted the Diaspora, the Inquisition, the Pogroms, the Holocaust in the past, and is going finally to sift them out during, rather than after, the Great Tribulation: *"Therefore thus saith the Lord GOD; Because ye are all become dross, behold, therefore I will gather you into the midst of Jerusalem. As they gather silver, and brass, and iron, and lead, and tin, into the midst of the furnace, to blow the fire upon it, to melt it; so will I gather you in mine anger and in my fury, and I will leave you there, and melt you. Yea, I will gather you, and blow upon you in the fire of my wrath, and ye shall be melted in the midst thereof. As silver is melted in the midst of the furnace, so shall ye be melted in the midst thereof; and ye shall know that I the LORD have poured out my fury upon you"* (Ezekiel 22:19-22). *"And it shall come to pass,*

that in all the land, saith the LORD, two parts therein shall be cut off and die; but the third shall be left therein. And I will bring the third part through the fire, and will refine them as silver is refined, and will try them as gold is tried: they shall call on my name, and I will hear them: I will say, It is my people: and they shall say, The LORD is my God" (Zechariah 13:8-9).

The repentance of the one third seems to occur shortly before, rather than following, the Lord's return, though commentators are not unanimous here, and I admit to having changed my view when researching 'The Minor Prophets And The End Times'. You can read of their very moving national, family and individual repentance in Zechariah chapter 12.

Those well-meaning Christians who portray Israel as already being well-nigh perfect do Jews a grave disservice. It is right that we should love them for the Lord's sake, defend them against Anti-Semitism, evangelise them when we can and pray for the peace of Jerusalem; but we must be aware that for that troubled nation revelation, repentance, revival and restoration still lie ahead within God's revealed programme.

UNPRECEDENTED, UNREPEATABLE TRIBULATION

Now what follows immediately in Matthew 24 and Revelation 12 is immensely important. *"For then shall be great tribulation, such as was not since the beginning of the world to this time, no, nor ever shall be. And except those days should be shortened, there should no flesh be saved: but for the elect's sake those days shall be shortened"* (Matthew 24:21-22). Jeremiah 30:7 describes it thus: *"Alas! for that day is great, so that none is like it: it is even the time of Jacob's trouble; but he shall be saved out of it."* Daniel foretells it too: *"And at that time shall Michael stand up, the great prince which standeth for the children of thy people: and there shall be a time of trouble, such as never was since there was a nation even to that same time: and at that time thy people shall be delivered, every one that shall be found written in the book"* (Daniel 12:1).

Michael is the only heavenly being identified as an archangel, though Satan was probably one before his fall. We find Michael again in Revelation 12: *"And there was war in heaven: Michael and his angels fought against the dragon; and the dragon fought and his angels, And prevailed not; neither was their place found any more in heaven. And the great dragon was cast out, that old serpent, called the Devil, and Satan, which deceiveth the whole world: he was cast out into the earth, and his angels were cast out with him"* (Revelation 12:7-9). Satan has never lived in Heaven since his fall; he has held the title of *'prince of the power of the air'* (Ephesians 2:2). But he has always had access since his rebellion and fall, which occurred either at the beginning of earth's history or possibly even before; some of his fallen angels also seem to have had such a right of access. He had once been the anointed cherub, Lucifer, the mightiest of all God's created beings, but down through the centuries he has been the malignant accuser of the brethren. Job 1:7-12 relates one example of this activity.

Now Satan has to be banished from Heaven forever, initially and briefly cast down only as far as the earth: *"And I heard a loud voice saying in heaven, Now is come salvation, and strength, and the kingdom of our God, and the power of his Christ: for the accuser of our brethren is cast down, which accused them before our God day and night. And they overcame him by the blood of the Lamb, and by the word of their testimony; and they loved not their lives unto the death. Therefore rejoice, ye heavens, and ye that dwell in them. Woe to the inhabiters of the earth and of the sea! for the devil is come down unto you, having great wrath, because he knoweth that he hath but a short time"* (Revelation 12:10-12). We are reminded of that immensely important fact, that the blood of the Lamb is the only means of our salvation, the only provision made by God for our sins and the only means of overcoming the Devil. To prefer *any* other means is the supreme insult to God and can never avail. Thus the Great Tribulation begins with the Devil's wrath; but it will finish with God's greater wrath.

FOUR OF SEVEN TRUMPETS
Before we look at the Dragon and his two human deputies, let us return to the seven trumpets, which are first announced in Revelation 8, and see what they entail – some of scientists' very worst fears are to be realised. We will see in due course that the seventh one takes us to Christ's return in power, but it is not actually stated when they are to start in relation to other events, neither can we be really sure about the timing of the others or whether they bridge the mid-point gap. The final three are also described as 'woes', and certainly appear to lie within the Great Tribulation. *"And I saw the seven angels which stood before God; and to them were given seven trumpets. And another angel came and stood at the altar, having a golden censer; and there was given unto him much incense, that he should offer it with the prayers of all saints upon the golden altar which was before the throne. And the smoke of the incense, which came with the prayers of the saints, ascended up before God out of the angel's hand. And the angel took the censer, and filled it with fire of the altar, and cast it into the earth: and there were voices, and thunderings, and lightnings, and an earthquake"* (Revelation 8:2-5). For thousands of years oppressed men and women have wondered why God has not avenged them; even the Psalm writer questioned God. God listens and forgets nothing; but His timing is infinitely wiser than ours, and one day, looking back, we will fully understand that. The Apostle Paul was perceptive: *"For I reckon that the sufferings of this present time are not worthy to be compared with the glory which shall be revealed in us"* (Romans 8:18). In God's time His suffering saints will

be avenged. The Trumpet judgments are partly God's response to these pleas.

"And the seven angels which had the seven trumpets prepared themselves to sound. The first angel sounded, and there followed hail and fire mingled with blood, and they were cast upon the earth: and the third part of trees was burnt up, and all green grass was burnt up. And the second angel sounded, and as it were a great mountain burning with fire was cast into the sea: and the third part of the sea became blood; And the third part of the creatures which were in the sea, and had life, died; and the third part of the ships were destroyed. And the third angel sounded, and there fell a great star from heaven, burning as it were a lamp, and it fell upon the third part of the rivers, and upon the fountains of waters; And the name of the star is called Wormwood: and the third part of the waters became wormwood; and many men died of the waters, because they were made bitter. And the fourth angel sounded, and the third part of the sun was smitten, and the third part of the moon, and the third part of the stars; so as the third part of them was darkened, and the day shone not for a third part of it, and the night likewise" (Revelation 8:6-12).

Do these verses really need any explanation? No interval between them is stated, but a quick calculation based on limited data available suggests that they cannot reasonably be much more than six months apart, and could be considerably less; they could come in quick succession. I cannot get excited by conservation measures being taken by sincere people trying to 'save the planet'. All Christians should be fully aware that fundamentally 'saving the planet' entails first dealing with sin. Towards the end of this book we will see how God will RESTORE, rather than SAVE our physical environment. Whatever has happened to faith?

The aged Apostle has described to the best of His ability what he witnessed from Heaven, looking down to earth. The first trumpet suggests extreme atmospheric and ecological disasters perhaps occasioned by volcanoes. So much for fruit crops! It could all so easily happen, could it not? The sounding of the second trumpet introduces what seems to be a huge meteorite or asteroid. Already sensitive instruments are able to track such objects in the solar system; a scheduled one passed very close to the earth in November 2011. The outcome is precisely what scientists would expect. John sees one third of the earth being affected. This might relate to the Beast's empire or just imply that the whole earth will be affected proportionately. We now know how vulnerable the sea, once assumed to be inviolable, is.

The third trumpet seems to be similar – either an asteroid or a comet, with water supplies ruinously contaminated. The fourth tells of darkening of the sky, whether by smoke, volcanic ash or other means we can only surmise. The cumulative effect is similar to the third and fourth seals which we saw in the previous chapter. Famine and death will follow; stronger nations will plunder weaker nations for rapidly dwindling food supplies, and stronger families will plunder weaker ones. Lawlessness will abound.

TRUMPETS CALLED WOES

Eleven verses are devoted to the fifth trumpet, but we will pass over them fairly briefly. It is dangerous not to be fully aware of the powers of darkness, but it is unhealthy to be preoccupied with them. *"And the fifth angel sounded, and I saw a star fall from heaven unto the earth: and to him was given the key of the bottomless pit. And he opened the bottomless pit; and there arose a smoke out of the pit, as the smoke of a great furnace; and the sun and the air were darkened by reason of the smoke of the pit. And there came out of the smoke locusts upon the earth: and unto them was given power, as the scorpions of the earth have power.... And they had a king over them, which is the angel of the bottomless pit, whose name in the Hebrew tongue is Abaddon, but in the Greek tongue hath his name Apollyon"* (Revelation 9:1-3,11). Probably at the time that Satan is to be cast down, myriads of the most evil demons or fallen angels will be released to reinforce the Devil and his minions and to bring absolute misery upon earth's surviving inhabitants. Unlike those in the sixth trumpet they will be unable to slay men and women, but only torment them.

There have been quite enough of these fallen beings even in this present age to contend with without this future task force: *"For we wrestle not against flesh and blood, but against principalities, against powers, against the rulers of the darkness of this world, against spiritual wickedness in high places"* (Ephesians 6:12). God's people are expressly forbidden to make contact with occult forces which are described as deceivers. Tarot card, fortune telling, Ouija boards and lucky charms are not harmless fun, but totally unacceptable. God will never condone Christians who prefer not to keep all their spiritual eggs in one basket, so to speak; that suggests a lack of saving faith and is the supreme affront to the One who said: *"I am the way, the truth, and the life: no man cometh unto the Father, but by me"* (John 14:6). Jesus Christ demands our unconditional trust; supplementing Christian faith with other sources is anathema, as one young congregation was reminded by Paul (Galatians 1:6-8).

The portent of the sixth trumpet is probably the most difficult one to interpret; nine verses are devoted to it. This also is partly a response to the prayers of the oppressed: *"And the sixth angel sounded, and I heard a voice from the four horns of the golden altar which is before God, Saying to the sixth angel which had the trumpet, Loose the four angels which are bound in the great river Euphrates. And the four angels were loosed, which were prepared for an hour, and a day, and a month, and a year, for to slay the third part of men"* (Revelation 9:13-15). The horns of the altar were provided for refugees to hold onto when pursued; a merciful God always hears those who sincerely cry to Him. We learn in the closing chapter of Daniel much of the way in which God uses His angels to control nations and to defend His own people. We are rarely given details, but in many a campaign God must have said "So far, but no further!" The River Euphrates is often considered to be the boundary between the East and the West; it is the declared border of the Promised Land, though only at the end of King David's reign and in Solomon's time was this frontier achieved. It was also the easternmost limit of the Roman Empire at its greatest extent. During the Great Tribulation armies are to be allowed the freedom to invade. Some think that this may include a challenge by the Orient against the Beast and his empire. The A.V. suggests a single army of two hundred million; actually 'army' should be in the plural. This may or may not imply the sum total of two or more invasions.

"And thus I saw the horses in the vision, and them that sat on them, having breastplates of fire, and of jacinth, and brimstone: and the heads of the horses were as the heads of lions; and out of their mouths issued fire and smoke and brimstone. By these three was the third part of men killed, by the fire, and by the smoke, and by the brimstone, which issued out of their mouths. For their power is in their mouth, and in their tails: for their tails were like unto serpents, and had heads, and with them they do hurt" (Revelation 9:17-19).

Now it is not clear whether we have here men, demons, or men possessed by demons, or whether this is to be regarded as symbolic or whether it is John's way of describing modern weaponry. It does not matter at present, but it will matter enormously to those who turn to their Bibles in that dreadful day; they will be in no doubt as to how to interpret this section of a book of the Bible ignored by many today, but due to be invaluable then. Certainly China has boasted that she could put two hundred million troops in the field. And when one's crops are devastated and one is starving, the natural reaction is for the stronger nation to invade and plunder the weaker one. We are staggered by the death toll – one third of the world's by then already depleted population. For those who have already repented, death will seem preferable to continued earthly life. God will preserve some righteous people to continue witnessing and to be the basis of a future population following Jesus' return, as we shall see later.

Men and woman are capable of hardening their hearts beyond the ability to repent. Rejection of God is always self-imposed, and often there is no way back, as Esau discovered: *"He was rejected: for he found no place of repentance, though he sought it carefully with tears"* (Hebrews 12:17). The following two verses tell us of this happening, and of a persistent refusal to give up idolatry. It rather appears that during the Great Tribulation a variety of personal images, idols or other representations of the Beast will be venerated. The Ten Commandments banned such things, but they will apparently abound then, as will occult practices, whether or not drug induced; the word translated 'sorceries' implies drugs. *"And they did not repent of their murders or their sorceries or their sexual immorality or their thefts"* (Revelation 9:21 NKJV). As one would expect, the vulnerable will be mercilessly plundered in a world of extreme moral depravity.

THE SEVENTH TRUMPET

I avoid calling this the *last* trumpet, because some people, perhaps understandably, have confused this with the resurrection of Church saints: *"Behold, I tell you a mystery: We shall not all sleep, but we shall all be changed — in a moment, in the twinkling of an eye, at the last trumpet. For the trumpet will sound, and the dead will be raised incorruptible, and we shall be changed"* (I Corinthians 15:51-52 NKJV). Paul did **not** specify the *seventh* trumpet. The last trumpet of three was a well-known juncture for marching off in the Roman Army as it had been for the Children of Israel in their wilderness wanderings (Numbers 10:1-10). The future seven trumpets were unknown when Paul wrote; had he known of them, he might have talked about the Rapture as being at the 'third woe'. But He didn't; it will be anything but a woeful event!

Now, as we saw in the previous chapter, the seventh trumpet seems to take us right up to Christ's Return in Power, so we will be very brief here, simply taking time to conclude this little review of the seven trumpet blasts. *"The angel whom I saw standing on the sea and on the land raised up his hand to heaven and swore by Him who lives forever and ever, who created heaven and the things that are in it, the earth and the things that are in it, and the sea and the things that are in it, that there should be delay no longer, but in the days of the sounding of the seventh angel, when he is about to sound, the mystery of God would be finished, as He declared to His servants the prophets"* (Revelation 10:5-7 NKJV). The seventh trumpet blast seems to occupy some time, in contrast to the *'twinkling of an eye'* quoted earlier. The A.V. rendering, *"time shall be no more"*, in contrast with the better *"there should be no more delay"*, gave rise to a popular hymn, but is not a good translation; time as we know it will go on for at least a thousand years after this! Whatever the mystery referred to is, it cannot be the Church, which was never declared to the prophets. It seems that this is the age-old mystery of why God has not yet intervened in righteous judgment and when He will. It will be at the seventh trumpet blast: *"The second woe is past; and, behold, the third woe cometh quickly. And the seventh angel sounded; and there were great voices in heaven, saying, The kingdoms of this world are become the kingdoms of our Lord, and of his Christ; and he shall reign for ever and ever"* (Revelation 11:14-15). We shall return to these momentous events later.

THE TRINITY OF EVIL

In Revelation chapter 13 the three members of what is sometimes called the Trinity of Evil are presented together. Satan has already been aptly described in the previous chapter as *'the dragon'*, *'the serpent of old'* and *'the accuser of our brethren'*; other names are used elsewhere in Scripture. We saw earlier that the inhabitants of the world are to be warned when he is cast down among them, having great wrath, knowing that time is running out for him. Only from Revelation 13 onwards is it clear that there are to be two end-time Beasts, rather than just one. It is safer not to call either the Antichrist, because it may well be that the second Beast will conform to that description better than the first. Only in retrospect can the contrast between these persons be seen, as in the differing 'little horns' of Daniel chapters 7 and 8. These matters are too complex to investigate here. *"And I stood upon the sand of the sea, and saw a beast rise up out of the sea, having seven heads and ten horns, and upon his horns ten crowns, and upon his heads the name of blasphemy. And the beast which I saw was like unto a leopard, and his feet were as the feet of a bear, and his mouth as the mouth of a lion: and the dragon gave him his power, and his seat, and great authority. And I saw one of his heads as it were wounded to death; and his deadly wound was healed: and all the world wondered after the beast. And they worshipped the dragon which gave power unto the beast: and they worshipped the beast, saying, Who is like unto the beast? who is able to make war with him? And there was given unto him a mouth speaking great things and blasphemies; and power was given unto him to continue forty and two months. And he opened his mouth in blasphemy against God, to blaspheme his name, and his tabernacle, and them that dwell in heaven. And it was given unto him to make war with the saints, and to overcome them: and power was given him over all kindreds, and tongues, and nations. And all that dwell upon the earth shall worship him, whose names are not written in the book of life of the Lamb slain from the foundation of the world"* (Revelation 13:1-8).

The nations are sometimes likened to the restless sea; this First Beast seems almost certainly to be Gentile, in contrast to the Second Beast which arises from the land, which suggests Israel, making him a Jew, capable of convincing the unwary that he is their Messiah. Strictly speaking, then, he is the one best described as the Antichrist, but he is more often called the False Prophet in Revelation, and we will be using this title. The First Beast is the last world emperor of the broken sequence of five foretold to Nebuchadnezzar. This is an empire of ten subordinate kingdoms, each with its ruler. We will see more of these shortly. The lion, bear and leopard characteristics refer to former Babylonian. Medo-Persian and Grecian Empires, as is confirmed by comparing Daniel chapters 2 and 7. These were succeeded by the Roman Empire, so, if we recall that latter day empire which was to combine the iron of Rome with incompatible clay, we have a final empire, which shares the features of the previous empires and might incorporate the territories of both the old Eastern and Western Roman Empires. The Promised Land came of course within the Eastern half of the old empire and will have some sort of treaty or covenant relationship with it, as was the case in New Testament times when kings like Herod, Agrippa and Philip occupied lesser thrones, but were subject to Caesar. As we saw in our previous chapter, the covenant will be broken at the mid-point of the seven years, when the rebuilt Jerusalem Temple will be desecrated and an occult abomination set up within it.

This is where the Second Beast fits in: *"And I beheld another beast coming up out of the earth; and he had two horns like a lamb, and he spake as a dragon. And he exerciseth all the power of the first beast before him, and causeth the earth and them which dwell therein to worship the first beast, whose deadly wound was healed. And he doeth great wonders, so that he maketh fire come down from heaven on the earth in the sight of men, And deceiveth them that dwell on the earth by the means of those miracles which he had power to do in the sight of the beast; saying to them that dwell on the earth, that they should make an image to the beast, which had the wound by a sword, and did live. And he had power to give life unto the image of the beast, that the image of the beast should both speak, and cause that as many as would not worship the image of the beast should be killed"* (Revelation 13:11-15). This is a miracle working religious beast, hence the title False Prophet, parodying the Holy Spirit by directing worship to the First Beast. It rather appears that the First Beast is actually slain and resurrected, in mimicry of Jesus' resurrection. How and why this should happen must be subject to some speculation until it actually occurs. It is even suggested by some that the First Beast may be some historical figure brought back to life. We are not told all the answers and should keep an open mind here.

THE MARK OF THE BEAST
It is the False Prophet who will impose the universal Mark of the Beast in a centralised world economy. The Mark will be granted only to those who acknowledge the sovereignty and deity of the First Beast. *"And he causeth all, both small and great, rich and poor, free and bond, to receive a mark in their right hand, or in their foreheads: And that no man might buy or sell, save he that had the mark, or the name of the beast, or the number of his name"* (Revelation 13:16-17). Life without the Mark will be precarious indeed, yet God declares that those who receive it will place themselves forever beyond His mercy and salvation: *"And the third angel followed them, saying with a loud*

voice, If any man worship the beast and his image, and receive his mark in his forehead, or in his hand, The same shall drink of the wine of the wrath of God, which is poured out without mixture into the cup of his indignation; and he shall be tormented with fire and brimstone in the presence of the holy angels, and in the presence of the Lamb" (Revelation 14:9-10).

I take no pleasure and find it very difficult to record all this; but the Bible declares both good news and bad news, and to declare the one without the other in order to gain popularity and to make Christianity appear more 'inclusive' is utterly irresponsible for ministers of the Gospel. If we think about it, it must be so. The difficulty is that we tend to forget the awful cost to God of providing our free salvation. We have already seen that during the Beginning of Sorrows the whole world will have been saturated with the Gospel of the Kingdom – repentance leading to salvation - and now another quite unprecedented warning is given as men and women make their momentous decisions: *"And I saw another angel fly in the midst of heaven, having the everlasting gospel to preach unto them that dwell on the earth, and to every nation, and kindred, and tongue, and people, Saying with a loud voice, Fear God, and give glory to him; for the hour of his judgment is come: and worship him that made heaven, and earth, and the sea, and the fountains of waters"* (Revelation 14:6-7). God will on no account share His glory with Satan or his bestial deputies. The fountains of waters are probably singled out because extreme fresh and sea water pollution is to be a notable result of both trumpets and bowls of wrath. Quite how this angelic herald will appear we do not know.

ONE WORLD RELIGION?
Before this announcement of the third angel, we find another angel announcing: *"Babylon is fallen, is fallen, that great city, because she made all nations drink of the wine of the wrath of her*

fornication" (Revelation 14:8). This helps us to time the fall of Mystery Babylon, the subject of Revelation 17. All false religion is Satanic – it cannot be otherwise, and usually involves pride through upward striving rather than humble acceptance or, in some cases, supposed evolution towards deity, forgetting that Jesus Christ, the Son of God came all the way down, not merely half way, for us: *"Let this mind be in you which was also in Christ Jesus, who, being in the form of God, did not consider it robbery to be equal with God, but made Himself of no reputation, taking the form of a bondservant, and coming in the likeness of men. And being found in appearance as a man, He humbled Himself and became obedient to the point of death, even the death of the cross"* (Philippians 2:5-8 NKJV).

False religion can be traced back to Genesis chapters 10 and 11, to Nimrod and the Tower of Babel. Babylon's iniquity is ancient; God destroyed her ziggurat when, in defiance of God's command to disperse in the world which had emerged from the Flood, she sought to establish herself as a centralised occult headquarters (Genesis 11:4-9). Jeremiah's prophecy had both contemporary and end-time significance: *"Flee out of the midst of Babylon, and deliver every man his soul: be not cut off in her iniquity; for this is the time of the LORD'S vengeance; he will render unto her a recompence. Babylon hath been a golden cup in the LORD'S hand, that made all the earth drunken: the nations have drunken of her wine; therefore the nations are mad"* (Jeremiah 51:6-7).

Satan has ensured that a wide variety of personal achievement religion has been available to cater for every culture and taste. Even those practising a pure religion are in danger of being drawn in; we must ever be on our guard against compromise – and particularly pride, for Christianity forbids that we should boast: *"God forbid that I should glory, save in the cross of our Lord Jesus Christ"* (Galatians 6:14).

During the Middle Ages, a number of devout Roman Catholic scholars saw their own Church as being the Antichrist, and the Reformers were quick to take up the idea, the seven mountains of Revelation 17:9 being highly suggestive. Certainly Rome conformed to the martyring image, being guilty of innumerable deaths during the Inquisition and Counter Reformation. But Scripture distinguishes the fallen harlot religion from the individual end-time Beast and also from his empire. Moreover we may become so preoccupied with one imperfect form of what calls itself Christianity, that we easily become blinded to the apostasy of others. Moreover God still has people even in Babylon! *"And I heard another voice from heaven, saying, Come out of her, my people, that ye be not partakers of her sins, and that ye receive not of her plagues"* (Revelation 18:4).

It seems that during the Beginning of Sorrows false religion will reach its short-lived pinnacle of power, in all probability achieving an unprecedented amalgamation or breaking down of ancient inter-religious barriers and rivalries. Satan, having at last exhausted his use for them, will then dispense with the lot! The world is likely to applaud. Already overtures are being made by both Catholic and some Protestant leaders towards Islam, Buddhism and others. Some, even in Islam, are reciprocating, although this rarely makes news headlines. *"Then one of the seven angels who had the seven bowls came and talked with me, saying to me, 'Come, I will show you the judgment of the great harlot who sits on many waters, with whom the kings of the earth committed fornication, and the inhabitants of the earth were made drunk with the wine of her fornication.' So he carried me away in the Spirit into the wilderness. And I saw a woman sitting on a scarlet beast which was full of names of blasphemy, having seven heads and ten horns. The woman was arrayed in purple and scarlet, and adorned with gold and precious stones and pearls, having in her hand a golden cup full of abominations and the filthiness of her fornication. And on her forehead a name was written: MYSTERY, BABYLON THE GREAT, THE MOTHER OF HARLOTS AND OF THE ABOMINATIONS OF THE EARTH. I saw the woman, drunk with the blood of the saints and with the blood of the martyrs of Jesus. And when I saw her, I marveled with great amazement"* (Revelation 17:1-6 NKJV). If that old Apostle who had walked and talked on earth with Jesus marvelled, we can hardly be blamed for being astonished by the last flowering of the world's multi-faith monstrosity. In our next chapter we will see the slightly later destruction of the political and commercial Babylon the Great.

SATAN IN HIS TRUE COLOURS

The influence of religious leaders over the affairs of men and even over kings and emperors has always been formidable. With all true believers, the salt of the earth, caught up to Heaven at the Rapture, restraint will have gone and this religious horror will have been free from her main source of opposition. Rarely has Satan dared openly to reveal his true identity; in most religions he has permitted a veneer of respectability and sacrosanctity. Satan has always appeared in disguise except in overt devil worship and, of course, long ago, when he tempted Jesus in the wilderness (Matthew 4:1, Luke 4:3). Him he could not deceive.

At last Satan is going to be able to free himself from all sham and dispense with what has served him well for thousands of year. At last both personally and in the form of his two Beasts, he will direct all worship on earth to himself. The first Beast, as last in the line of emperors, will, with the acquiescence of his ten subordinate kings or rulers, turn and rend the harlot church which had helped them to power: *"And the ten horns which thou sawest are ten kings, which have received no kingdom as yet; but receive power as kings one hour with the beast. These have one mind, and shall give their power and strength unto the beast..... And he saith unto me, The waters which thou sawest, where the whore sitteth, are peoples, and multitudes, and nations, and tongues. And the ten horns which thou sawest upon the beast, these shall hate the whore, and shall make her desolate and naked, and shall eat her flesh, and burn her with fire. For God hath put in their hearts to fulfil his will, and to agree, and give their kingdom unto the beast, until the words of God shall be fulfilled"* (Revelation 17:12-13, 15-17). Referring to the Day of the Lord, or Day of Vengeance of our God, as Isaiah calls it, Paul writes: *"Let no one deceive you in any way; for that day will not come, unless the rebellion comes first, and the man of lawlessness is revealed, the son of perdition, who opposes and exalts himself against every so-called god or object of worship, so that he takes his seat in the temple of God, proclaiming himself to be God"* (II Thessalonians 2:3-4 RSV). We quoted that earlier, but it needs to be repeated here. Perhaps, having thus publicly and blasphemously desecrated the Holy of Holies in the Jerusalem Temple, he will, when he himself is absent, simply be represented there by the hideous image which Jesus called the Abomination of Desolation (Matthew 24:15, Mark 13:14); Revelation 13 seems to indicate that this will be so.

BOWLS OF WRATH

As the Great Tribulation takes its short course, there will be more and more wars. Daniel 11: 36-45 tells of the later ones in the Middle East. Dreadful though the judgments following the sounding of the first five trumpets will be, the Bowls (or Vials in the A.V.) of Wrath during the latter part of the Great Tribulation will be three times more intense than the Trumpet judgments, and will be world-wide. These follow the public plea to Christ to reap earth's over-ripe harvest and vintage: *"And I looked, and behold a white cloud, and upon the cloud one sat like unto the Son of man, having on his head a golden crown, and in his hand a sharp sickle And another angel came out of the temple, crying with a loud voice to him that sat on the cloud, Thrust in thy sickle, and reap: for the time is come for thee to reap; for the harvest of the earth is ripe..... And another angel came out from the altar, which had power over fire; and cried with a loud cry to him that had the sharp sickle, saying, Thrust in thy sharp sickle, and gather the clusters of the vine of the earth; for her grapes are fully ripe"* (Revelation 14:14,15,18). Revelation chapter 16 tells us of the outpouring of these bowls of wrath, which are similar in many respects to the trumpets, except with regards to intensity. The world will indeed come to the brink of annihilation, just as Jesus promised (Matthew 24:22). We will leave the sixth and seventh bowls until our next chapter, as they take us on to Armageddon and Christ's return in power.

CHAPTER FIVE

King of Kings and Lord of Lords

ANTICIPATED ANNIHILATION

We ended Chapter 4 before the pouring out of the 6th Bowl of Wrath, having already seen five seals opened and heard six trumpets sounded. We are almost at the end of the Great Tribulation in our end-time studies. This is the summary in Mark's Gospel: *"For in those days there will be tribulation, such as has not been since the beginning of the creation which God created until this time, nor ever shall be. And unless the Lord had shortened those days, no flesh would be saved; but for the elect's sake, whom He chose, He shortened the days"* (Mark 13:19-20 NKJV). The Lord's personal and visible intervention will be an act of mercy, therefore, as well as one of judgment – intervention in the nick of time, as one might say. The Gospels devote most of their text to what happened in a space of little more than three years at Jesus First Coming, having most to say about the climax of His life on earth. So we need not be surprised that elsewhere in the Bible so much space is devoted to events relating to His Second Coming, and particularly to its climax. So much has got to happen in a very short space of time. We must appreciate that fitting everything revealed to us into the correct sequence is probably impossible, and opinions may differ a little. Some things are likely to happen consecutively and some simultaneously. Differentiating in advance between cause and effect is not always easy.

It will be a ruinously devastated world, almost incapable of sustaining life. Tectonic movements and climate changes of ever increasing intensity will have resulted in tsunamis, hurricanes, volcanic ash clouds, lethal pollution on a planetary scale and much more. Mankind will have become sharply divided into (a) those who have pledged loyalty to Satan and his man, and become incapable of natural affection and compassion, and put themselves forever beyond repentance and (b) those who, at the risk of martyrdom, have repented and turned to Christ through the preaching of the Gospel of the Kingdom. There will of course be some Jews who have been granted a wilderness refuge, but these will be a tiny minority, one feels. Also there will be a number of Jewish heroes who will be divinely empowered to defend their city against assaults by neighbouring lands shortly before Armageddon (Zechariah 12:1-9). We saw in our Chapter 4 that Michael the Archangel will be tasked to defend God's ancient Covenant people. (Daniel 12:1). *"For it is the day of the LORD'S vengeance, the year of recompense for the cause of Zion"* (Isaiah 34:8 NKJV).

COMMERCIAL CATASTROPHE

As we have seen, the ultimate apostate multi-faith religious harlot, Mystery Babylon, will have been discarded more than three years earlier and replaced by virtually undisguised Devil worship. The Devil's 'P.R.' will be exceedingly convincing to those who are determined to reject God. But Babylon the Great will survive almost to the end; it is described in Revelation 18. A World Trade Centre was demolished on 9/11, but a different and infamous one is to reach the peak of its iniquity during the Great Tribulation. The current commercial, economic and monetary instability would provide an ideal opportunity for the Beast to impose his authority and bolster his prestige by centralising and stabilising this global disarray. It is described in words which may now seem archaic, but had to make some sense to readers over the past nineteen centuries. Whether a new city will arise on the Plains of Shinar near Babylon is uncertain; Genesis 11:2 and Zechariah 4:5-11 suggest that it might, and Saddam Hussein did much building there in preparation for his own personal but thwarted ambitions. It might simply refer to the economic structure. Either way, it will be merciless and ruthless, devoid of compassion and common decency, fuelled by unleashed passions and greed, with total disregard for employees, customers, the vulnerable and even the lives and souls of fellow beings; people will be mere commodities. Already we see in what were once Christian countries, moral restrictions imposed by traditional values being cast off as increasingly irrelevant. Surely this age is swiftly coming to a close!

Its sudden fate is graphically described. It does not require me to point out how far we are already on the road to this Babylon the Great. Unrestrained Communism and Capitalism, which have seemed to be poles apart, when devoid of inhibitions and fired by human greed, are capable of completing the full circle and meeting at a point of depravity at which their destruction at their Creator's hand becomes inevitable: *"And the great city was divided into three parts, and the cities of the nations fell: and great Babylon came in remembrance before God, to give unto her the cup of the wine of the fierceness of his wrath"* (Revelation 16:19). It will be one of the preliminary happenings of the Lord's Return. The Heavens will rejoice; men will bewail it: *"Alas, alas, that great city, that was clothed in fine linen, and purple, and scarlet, and decked with gold, and precious stones, and pearls! For in one hour so great riches is come to nought..... Rejoice over her, thou heaven, and ye holy apostles and prophets; for God hath avenged you on her..... And in her was found the blood of prophets, and of saints, and of all that were slain upon the earth"* (Revelation

18:16,17,20,24). Mercy is a lovely quality, but there are times when it is not appropriate.

TECTONIC TORTURE

In Chapter 3 we saw that the seven Seals, Trumpets and Bowls of Wrath all take us to the Lord's Return. We can let Scripture speak for itself and keep comments to a minimum: *"And I beheld when he had opened the sixth seal, and, lo, there was a great earthquake; and the sun became black as sackcloth of hair, and the moon became as blood; And the stars of heaven fell unto the earth, even as a fig tree casteth her untimely figs, when she is shaken of a mighty wind. And the heaven departed as a scroll when it is rolled together; and every mountain and island were moved out of their places. And the kings of the earth, and the great men, and the rich men, and the chief captains, and the mighty men, and every bondman, and every free man, hid themselves in the dens and in the rocks of the mountains; And said to the mountains and rocks, Fall on us, and hide us from the face of him that sitteth on the throne, and from the wrath of the Lamb: For the great day of his wrath is come; and who shall be able to stand?"* (Revelation 6:12-17). The sixth seal is the last one which signals anything happening on earth; the seventh takes us to Heaven to see the trumpets being prepared to be sounded. When the Lord Jesus Christ leaves Heaven, men and women on earth will be given a unique glimpse of the Heavenly throne and recognise that the coming Judge is the once crucified Lamb of God, whose saving sacrifice they have disdained. By then it will be too late to repent, and people will know it and tremble.

"And the seventh angel sounded; and there were great voices in heaven, saying, The kingdoms of this world are become the kingdoms of our Lord, and of his Christ; and he shall reign for ever and ever. And the four and twenty elders, which sat before God on their seats, fell upon their faces, and worshipped God, Saying, We

give thee thanks, O Lord God Almighty, which art, and wast, and art to come; because thou hast taken to thee thy great power, and hast reigned. And the nations were angry, and thy wrath is come, and the time of the dead, that they should be judged, and that thou shouldest give reward unto thy servants the prophets, and to the saints, and them that fear thy name, small and great; and shouldest destroy them which destroy the earth" (Revelation 11:15-18). Those in Heaven, whose comprehension will not have become distorted or embittered, will recognise the unassailable righteousness of God's timely intervention.

"And the seventh angel poured out his vial into the air; and there came a great voice out of the temple of heaven, from the throne, saying, It is done. And there were voices, and thunders, and lightnings; and there was a great earthquake, such as was not since men were upon the earth, so mighty an earthquake, and so great….. And every island fled away, and the mountains were not found" (Revelation 16:17-18,20). However much we may value our 'priceless heritage', God will one day clear it all away, to replace it with something pure and holy and incomparably better. Then we will have no pangs of regret such as we might have now.

Perhaps John recalled the earlier prophecy of Isaiah: *"The earth is utterly broken down, the earth is clean dissolved, the earth is moved exceedingly. The earth shall reel to and fro like a drunkard, and shall be removed like a cottage; and the transgression thereof shall be heavy upon it; and it shall fall, and not rise again. And it shall come to pass in that day, that the LORD shall punish the host of the high ones that are on high, and the kings of the earth upon the earth. And they shall be gathered together, as prisoners are gathered in the pit, and shall be shut up in the prison, and after many days shall they be visited. Then the moon shall be confounded, and the sun ashamed, when the LORD of hosts shall reign in mount Zion, and in Jerusalem, and before his ancients gloriously"* (Isaiah

24:19-23). The NKJV's 'hut', as opposed to the AV's 'cottage' is more appropriate. This is very descriptive of a planet subject to asteroid strikes or similar phenomena. In a prophecy of which only the first phase was initially fulfilled on the Day of Pentecost (Acts 2:17-20), Joel said: *"And also upon the servants and upon the handmaids in those days will I pour out my spirit. And I will shew wonders in the heavens and in the earth, blood, and fire, and pillars of smoke. The sun shall be turned into darkness, and the moon into blood, before the great and the terrible day of the LORD come"* (Joel 2:29-31).

MILITARY MADNESS
We have already seen something of the restraining angels at the sixth Trumpet removing the ancient Euphrates obstacle. The sixth Bowl reveals Satan, through his demon recruiters, amassing the armies from around the world. But this is to be permitted only within the controlling sovereign will of Almighty God. Sound military strategy and common sense do not come into it; the armies will be demon driven: *"Then the sixth angel poured out his bowl on the great river Euphrates, and its water was dried up, so that the way of the kings from the east might be prepared. And I saw three unclean spirits like frogs coming out of the mouth of the dragon, out of the mouth of the beast, and out of the mouth of the false prophet. For they are spirits of demons, performing signs, which go out to the kings of the earth and of the whole world, to gather them to the battle of that great day of God Almighty. 'Behold, I am coming as a thief. Blessed is he who watches, and keeps his garments, lest he walk naked and they see his shame.' And they gathered them together to the place called in Hebrew, Armageddon"* (Revelation 16:12-16). It is God, not generals, who will choose the battle field. When we look at Revelation 19:19, we will see that this confrontation is envisaged as a crazy and outrageous direct attack on the Lord Jesus Christ and God's city of Jerusalem. But God allows the vanguard to advance only as far as Armageddon, the wide,

now irrigated and intensively cultivated valley in northern Israel north of Mount Carmel. Christian friends and I, visiting a few years ago, were very moved, knowing that we would witness this battle not from earth, but from the air! *"Therefore wait ye upon me, saith the LORD, until the day that I rise up to the prey: for my determination is to gather the nations, that I may assemble the kingdoms, to pour upon them mine indignation, even all my fierce anger: for all the earth shall be devoured with the fire of my jealousy"* (Zephaniah 3:8). Note that Jesus Christ Himself interjects warnings to be ready in His Olivet Discourse. We do not have to await the armies amassing for Armageddon; our home-call will be sudden and unexpected, so that we may eventually be numbered among the heavenly host who will follow their descending Lord.

CONQUERING CHRIST

And now we come to one of the most august moments in this old planet's history. He who came to be *"A Man of Sorrows and acquainted with grief"* (Isaiah 53:3) is now revealed as *King of Kings and Lord of Lords*. John records: *"And I saw heaven opened, and behold a white horse; and he that sat upon him was called Faithful and True, and in righteousness he doth judge and make war. His eyes were as a flame of fire, and on his head were many crowns; and he had a name written, that no man knew, but he himself. And he was clothed with a vesture dipped in blood: and his name is called The Word of God. And the armies which were in heaven followed him upon white horses, clothed in fine linen, white and clean. And out of his mouth goeth a sharp sword, that with it he should smite the nations: and he shall rule them with a rod of iron: and he treadeth the winepress of the fierceness and wrath of Almighty God"* (Revelation 19:11-15). Here is irrefutable evidence that the Second Coming does not mark the end of the world, as the old myth claims. Jesus Christ is coming back to reign!

It would be lovely to take time to quote in full all the other texts which foretell this wonderful event, but let us look briefly at a couple: *"Then shall the LORD go forth, and fight against those nations, as when he fought in the day of battle. And his feet shall stand in that day upon the mount of Olives, which is before Jerusalem on the east, and the mount of Olives shall cleave in the midst thereof toward the east and toward the west, and there shall be a very great valley; and half of the mountain shall remove toward the north, and half of it toward the south"* (Zechariah 14:3-4). This is what will happen when Jesus comes back to earth. He will be seen at Armageddon, but His feet will alight on the Mount of Olives a little to the east of Jerusalem. Geologists have found a major fault line in precisely the prophesied position. *"And while they looked stedfastly toward heaven as he went up, behold, two men stood by them in white apparel; Which also said, Ye men of Galilee, why stand ye gazing up into heaven? this same Jesus, which is taken up from you into heaven, shall so come in like manner as ye have seen him go into heaven. Then returned they unto Jerusalem from the mount called Olivet"* (Acts 1:10-12). The Revelation account continues: *"And I saw the beast, and the kings of the earth, and their armies, gathered together to make war against him that sat on the horse, and against his army* (19:19).

ENEMIES ELIMINATED

"And the beast was taken, and with him the false prophet that wrought miracles before him, with which he deceived them that had received the mark of the beast, and them that worshipped his image. These both were cast alive into a lake of fire burning with brimstone. And the remnant were slain with the sword of him that sat upon the horse, which sword proceeded out of his mouth: and all the fowls were filled with their flesh" (Revelation 19:20-21). Zechariah tells us more of the fate of the combatants: *"And this shall be the plague wherewith the LORD will smite all the people that have fought against Jerusalem; Their flesh shall*

consume away while they stand upon their feet, and their eyes shall consume away in their holes, and their tongue shall consume away in their mouth" (14:12). Isaiah says: *"For, behold, the LORD will come with fire, and with his chariots like a whirlwind, to render his anger with fury, and his rebuke with flames of fire. For by fire and by his sword will the LORD plead with all flesh: and the slain of the LORD shall be many"* (Isaiah 66:15-16). It is the Beast and False prophet whose fate is to be swiftest. There will be no appeal, and apparently no formal sentence.

It is a great pity that there is a chapter division in Revelation between 19 and 20. Some have assumed that the narrative is broken here, but it certainly is not: *"And I saw an angel come down from heaven, having the key of the bottomless pit and a great chain in his hand. And he laid hold on the dragon, that old serpent, which is the Devil, and Satan, and bound him a thousand years. And cast him into the bottomless pit, and shut him up, and set a seal upon him, that he should deceive the nations no more, till the thousand years should be fulfilled: and after that he must be loosed a little season"* (Revelation 20:1-3). There can be no more secure prison than this. This is the first of six mentions of the thousand years, which is to be a tempter-free Millennium. Currently Satan is anything but bound *"Be sober, be vigilant; because your adversary the devil, as a roaring lion, walketh about, seeking whom he may devour"* I Peter 5:8). The very good reason for Satan's rather surprising brief release a thousand years later will be explained in our next chapter.

SEGREGATED SURVIVORS
During the Church Age Jew and Gentile have been able to become members of the Church, having all barriers between them removed, though without in any way stopping Christian Jews remaining Jews! (Ephesians 2:11-18, Romans 11:1 etc). But following the Rapture of the Church, God will differentiate between the two groups, as He who created

DNA is able to, because He has a special purpose for Israel in the future. *"Thus saith the LORD, which giveth the sun for a light by day, and the ordinances of the moon and of the stars for a light by night, which divideth the sea when the waves thereof roar; The LORD of hosts is his name: If those ordinances depart from before me, saith the LORD, then the seed of Israel also shall cease from being a nation before me for ever"* (Jeremiah 31:35-36). We saw in Chapter 4 in the section 'A Final Holocaust' how God would sift out the worthy of Israel so that they might enter their heritage in the Millennium.

Unrepentant Jews will evidently not survive to this point. Repentant ones will at last cry out in the words of the Psalm, sung by pilgrims on Palm Sunday but derided by the city: *"The stone which the builders refused is become the head stone of the corner. This is the LORD'S doing; it is marvellous in our eyes. This is the day which the LORD hath made; we will rejoice and be glad in it. Save now, I beseech thee, O LORD: O LORD, I beseech thee, send now prosperity. Blessed be he that cometh in the name of the LORD"* (Psalm 118:22-26). The conditions of that, *"Ye shall not see me henceforth until....."* of Matthew 23:39, which we quoted in an earlier chapter, will at last be met.

Isaiah describes tenderly this homecoming following the horrors of the Tribulation: *"He will swallow up death in victory; and the Lord GOD will wipe away tears from off all faces; and the rebuke of his people shall he take away from off all the earth: for the LORD hath spoken it. And it shall be said in that day, Lo, this is our God; we have waited for him, and he will save us: this is the LORD; we have waited for him, we will be glad and rejoice in his salvation"* (Isaiah 25:8-9). *"And it shall come to pass in that day, that the great trumpet shall be blown, and they shall come which were ready to perish in the land of Assyria, and the outcasts in the land of Egypt, and shall worship the LORD in the holy mount at Jerusalem"* (Isaiah 27:13). Much nonsense is taught about the

Church having forever replaced Israel; what Isaiah wrote can by no stretch of imagination be applied to the Church: *"For thy Maker is thine husband; the LORD of hosts is his name; and thy Redeemer the Holy One of Israel; The God of the whole earth shall he be called. For the LORD hath called thee as a woman forsaken and grieved in spirit, and a wife of youth, when thou wast refused, saith thy God. For a small moment have I forsaken thee; but with great mercies will I gather thee. In a little wrath I hid my face from thee for a moment; but with everlasting kindness will I have mercy on thee, saith the LORD thy Redeemer"* (Isaiah 54:5-8). The Church has never been *"as a woman forsaken"*. This time the return will be permanent: *"And I will plant them upon their land, and they shall no more be pulled up out of their land which I have given them, saith the LORD thy God"* (Amos 9:15).

Here the Lord Himself foretells their final recall. *"But immediately after the tribulation of those days the sun shall be darkened, and the moon not give her light, and the stars shall fall from heaven, and the powers of the heavens shall be shaken. And then shall appear the sign of the Son of man in heaven; and then shall all the tribes of the land lament, and they shall see the Son of man coming on the clouds of heaven with power and great glory. And he shall send his angels with a great sound of trumpet, and they shall gather together his elect from the four winds, from the one extremity of the heavens to the other extremity of them"* (Matthew 24:29-31 JND). Some translations say 'heaven' in that last sentence, but the Greek word can also mean atmosphere, and the sense is 'from wherever they are in the world'. With transport infrastructure, road, rail, tunnels, bridges and airfields destroyed, not to mention the poor physical state of these people, God will use his swifter and more certain angelic shepherds to bring them in. The resurrected saints in Heaven will already have followed their Lord: *"And Enoch also, the seventh from Adam, prophesied of these, saying, Behold, the Lord cometh with ten thousands of his saints To execute judgment upon all"* (Jude 1:14-15). The word 'elect' is often, though not exclusively applied to Israel; it must be here, because we are about to see how the Gentile survivors are dealt with separately, and it is Jesus Christ Himself, not angels, who will do the segregating.

GREAT GENTILE GATHERING

Here is a passage which some have described as the 'Parable of the Sheep and Goats' but it is no parable; a simile is used by our Lord to describe His future segregation of the Gentile survivors of the Great Tribulation. This is clearly stated by Him to be on earth, so it must not be confused with the very different last judgment, when the world has passed away. That we will see in our final chapter. Note that Jesus Christ describes Himself as the King in His Millennial reign which is now beginning. To the Church He is primarily Lord and Bridegroom, most precious relationships; the Church collectively is still the Bride.

The timing is clear enough; the context is so important. If we fail to appreciate that this is to follow the Great Tribulation, we will be totally confused. These survivors will have heard the Gospel preached by God's persecuted Tribulation witnesses and will either have accepted or rejected it. Rejection, as we have seen, will have involved accepting the Mark of the Beast and irrevocably declining God's mercy. I have devoted considerable space to this passage in 'The End Times In The Gospels', so will be very brief here. I recommend reading Matthew 25:31-46 in full; here are some extracts: *"When the Son of man shall come in his glory, and all the holy angels with him, then shall he sit upon the throne of his glory: And before him shall be gathered all nations: and he shall separate them one from another, as a shepherd divideth his sheep from the goats: And he shall set the sheep on his right hand, but the goats on the left. Then shall the King say unto them on his right hand, Come, ye blessed of my Father, inherit the kingdom prepared for you from the foundation of the world..... Then shall he say also unto them on the left hand, Depart from me, ye cursed, into everlasting fire..... And these shall go away into everlasting punishment: but the righteous into life eternal"* (Matthew 25:31-34,41,46).

The intermediate verses tell how those likened to sheep will have heeded and attended to God's evangelists, a very dangerous thing to do when the earth is under the sway of the Beast and False Prophet. This is not about how good deeds, compassion and charity, admirable though they may be, can merit eternal life. Works can never, never, never save, even though those done in Jesus' name will one day be rewarded. The 'sheep' are to enter the restored Millennial earth, of which we will see more in our next chapter; they will already be saved for eternity.

The location of this solemn assize seems to be in what we now call the Kedron Valley, between the Mount of Olives and Jerusalem, although this prophecy may refer to events immediately beforehand: *"Let the heathen be wakened, and come up to the valley of Jehoshaphat: for there will I sit to judge all the heathen round about. Put ye in the sickle, for the harvest is ripe: come, get you down; for the press is full, the fats overflow; for their wickedness is great. Multitudes, multitudes in the valley of decision: for the day of the LORD is near in the valley of decision"* (Joel 3:12-14).

RESURRECTED TO REIGN
Another most significant event following Christ's Return in Power is the resurrection of those from before the Church Age and those following it, in other words Old Testament saints and Tribulation martyrs. They are described separately and we are not told in which order of priority. What we do

know is that they are considered part of the First Resurrection, of which Jesus was the Firstfruits and the Church the main harvest: *"Blessed and holy is he that hath part in the first resurrection: on such the second death hath no power, but they shall be priests of God and of Christ, and shall reign with him a thousand years"* (Revelation 20:6).

Godly people in Old Testament times were confident of a future bodily resurrection: *"I know that my redeemer liveth, and that he shall stand at the latter day upon the earth. And though after my skin worms destroy this body, yet in my flesh shall I see God* (Job 19:25-26). An angel told Daniel: *"But go thou thy way till the end be: for thou shalt rest, and stand in thy lot at the end of the days"* (Daniel 12:13). The timing of their resurrection is indicated by Ezekiel: *"Therefore prophesy and say unto them, Thus saith the Lord GOD; Behold, O my people, I will open your graves, and cause you to come up out of your graves, and bring you into the land of Israel. And ye shall know that I am the LORD, when I have opened your graves, O my people, and brought you up out of your graves..... And shall put my spirit in you, and ye shall live, and I shall place you in your own land: then shall ye know that I the LORD have spoken it, and performed it, saith the LORD"* (Ezekiel 37:12,14). They will not have been included in the Rapture, where Heaven, not the Holy Land, is the immediate destination.

"I saw the souls of them that were beheaded for the witness of Jesus, and for the word of God, and which had not worshipped the beast, neither his image, neither had received his mark upon their foreheads, or in their hands; and they lived and reigned with Christ a thousand years" (Revelation 20:4). Earlier, as the sixth seal is opened, John records: *"I saw under the altar the souls of them that were slain for the word of God, and for the testimony which they held: And they cried with a loud voice, saying, How long, O Lord, holy and true, dost thou not judge and avenge our blood on*

them that dwell on the earth? And white robes were given unto every one of them; and it was said unto them, that they should rest yet for a little season, until their fellowservants also and their brethren, that should be killed as they were, should be fulfilled" (Revelation 6:9-11). Their wait is now over. Just as the Church had been resurrected collectively rather than individually, so it will be with the resurrection martyrs as a group. Thus the final stage of the first resurrection is now complete. In our next chapter we will see a little of what the Bible tells us about these wonderful future thousand years, which have sometimes been described as earth's Sabbath.

CHAPTER SIX

Earth's Golden Age

NEED FOR CLARITY

All Christians more or less believe in what is called 'life after death'. Some beliefs are Bible based, but not necessarily within context; others have little or nothing to do with reality, like being turned into angels or sitting on clouds playing harps throughout eternity! We have already seen what the Bible has to say about the status of the redeemed before and after the Rapture and know that we will follow our Saviour, Lord, Bridegroom and King of Kings when He returns in Power to destroy His enemies and to reign with a rod of iron. We have also seen how many redeemed, both Jews and Gentiles, will be permitted to enter the glorious Millennial kingdom in their mortal bodies. But what then? Those who do not believe in a future Millennium are confused about these matters, and tend to shy clear of them. Some see all the Millennial prophecies as different 'pictures of Heaven'. No wonder they are confused, because they so often conflict with what we are actually told elsewhere about Heaven. One encounters extraordinary statements even in popular hymns, such as, "Heaven and earth shall flee away, when He comes to reign". How can this be?

It is the Father's will that His Son has to reign where once He was rejected: *"Yet have I set my king upon my holy hill of Zion. I will declare the decree: the LORD hath said unto me, Thou art my Son; this day have I begotten thee. Ask of me, and I shall give thee the heathen for thine inheritance, and the uttermost parts of the earth for thy possession. Thou shalt break them with a rod of iron; thou shalt dash them in pieces like a potter's vessel"* (Psalm 2:6-9). That has never happened yet, but it most certainly will happen when He returns.

We shall look at five different aspect of the Millennium:
1. Christ worshipped – because He is God.
2. Christ reigning – because He is Man.
3. Resurrected saints in the Millennium, whether Old Testament, Church Age or Tribulation.
4. Those entering the Millennium in their mortal bodies, and their offspring.
5. The restored planet.

Perhaps we could call this the priority order. However I propose now to tackle these in reverse order to build up a picture of this wonderful time. The problem is that we have such a wealth of texts to choose from. The following is a list of passages, including some whole chapters, which mainly or exclusively concern the Millennium: Psalm 72; Isaiah 11; Isaiah 35; Isaiah 65:18-25; Jeremiah 31:23-37; Ezekiel chapters 40-48; Micah 4:1-8, Zechariah 14:14-21; Revelation 21:9 to 22:5. We will quote only briefly from these, but readers may wish to explore further; the Ezekiel and Revelation passages are probably not the best start points.

THE RESTORED PLANET
Millennial texts are virtually absent from the New Testament epistles, which concern the Church Age. It seems that before the Flood atmospheric conditions were entirely different: *"The LORD God had not caused it to rain upon the earth, and there was not a man to till the ground. But there went up a mist from the earth, and watered the whole face of the ground"* (Genesis 2:5-6) The Flood narrative tells how what was apparently a

great suspended water canopy, which had provided a global equable climate, suddenly descended at God's command. Many of the puzzles facing geographers, geologists and other specialists are explained if this startling fact is understood.

In our previous chapter we saw something of the unimaginable seismic and tectonic upheaval at the end of the Great Tribulation; the earth has previously endured something similar. I am among those who believe that this happened beneath the waters of the Flood, when deepest sea beds were elevated to mountain tops, and vice-versa, in the global fracturing, folding and buckling of the planet's surface. Admittedly I studied geomorphology only to first year degree level, but I know of eminent Christian scholars who understand the full significance of the Flood. What a wonderful but rather different world emerged under its Creator's direction. A similar reshaping could happen again when the remnants of earth's population are concentrated in one area around Jerusalem, which could be a safe haven. Jesus may not in fact have been talking figuratively when He said to His disciples: *"If ye have faith as a grain of mustard seed, ye shall say unto this mountain, Remove hence to yonder place; and it shall remove; and nothing shall be impossible unto you"* (Matthew 17:20). Jesus told them at another time that they would have unique responsibilities in resurrection; perhaps they are going to be privileged to share in the reconstruction of the devastated planet. Nothing is impossible. *"And the LORD shall utterly destroy the tongue of the Egyptian sea* (the Gulf of Aqaba); *and with his mighty wind shall he shake his hand over the river, and shall smite it in the seven streams, and make men go over dryshod"* (Isaiah 11:15). *"But in the last days it shall come to pass, that the mountain of the house of the LORD shall be established in the top of the mountains, and it shall be exalted above the hills; and people shall flow unto it"* (Micah 4:1). We have already noted that the geology of old Jerusalem will be radically altered; there is no particular reason why the Millennial one will not be built on a mountain top, is there?

A restored ecology will be one of the features: *"In the wilderness shall waters break out, and streams in the desert. And the parched ground shall become a pool, and the thirsty land springs of water: in the habitation of dragons, where each lay, shall be grass with reeds and rushes"* (Isaiah 35:6-7). *"Behold, the days come, saith the LORD, that the plowman shall overtake the reaper, and the treader of grapes him that soweth seed; and the mountains shall drop sweet wine, and all the hills shall melt. And I will bring again the captivity of my people of Israel, and they shall build the waste cities, and inhabit them; and they shall plant vineyards, and drink the wine thereof; they shall also make gardens, and eat the fruit of them"* (Amos 9:13-14). The successful kibbutzim of the modern Israeli state are only a tiny foretaste of what will happen when labour will be sweet and always rewarding, and complex irrigation systems will be unnecessary. *"And it shall come to pass in that day, that the mountains shall drop down new wine, and the hills shall flow with milk, and all the rivers of Judah shall flow with waters, and a fountain shall come forth of the house of the LORD, and shall water the valley of Shittim"*. Isaiah 41:18-19 tells us more of this future fertility. Present despair for our planet may be well enough founded; but for believers it should be at best no more than short term.

Peace will characterise the Millennial earth at all levels: *"He maketh wars to cease unto the end of the earth; he breaketh the bow, and cutteth the spear in sunder; he burneth the chariot in the fire"* (Psalm 46:9). *"And he shall judge among the nations, and shall rebuke many people: and they shall beat their swords into plowshares, and their spears into pruninghooks: nation shall not lift up sword against nation, neither shall they learn war any more"* (Isaiah 2:4). *"The wolf also shall dwell with the lamb, and the*

*leopard shall lie down with the kid; and the calf and the young lion
and the fatling together; and a little child shall lead them. And the
cow and the bear shall feed; their young ones shall lie down together:
and the lion shall eat straw like the ox. And the sucking child shall
play on the hole of the asp, and the weaned child shall put his hand
on the cockatrice' den. They shall not hurt nor destroy in all my
holy mountain"* (Isaiah 11:6-9).

MORTALS IN THE MILLENNIUM

Resurrected saints will of course be immortal. The word
'mortal' is used to describe those Tribulation survivors,
whom the Lord has classed as sheep or *"blessed of My Father"*,
who have been welcomed to remain in the earth which will
have been restored. They will have children and repopulate
the world. Many will have suffered much, but He who long
ago presented His Messianic credentials with miracles
foreshadowing that future day, will leave none physically
impaired in any way: *"Say to them that are of a fearful heart, Be
strong, fear not: behold, your God will come with vengeance, even
God with a recompence; he will come and save you. Then the eyes of
the blind shall be opened, and the ears of the deaf shall be unstopped.
Then shall the lame man leap as an hart, and the tongue of the dumb
sing"* (Isaiah 35:4-6). But then the Day of Vengeance will be over
and the Year of My Redeemed will have arrived.

*"Thus saith the LORD of hosts; There shall yet old men and old
women dwell in the streets of Jerusalem, and every man with his
staff in his hand for very age. And the streets of the city shall be
full of boys and girls playing in the streets thereof"* (Zechariah
8:4-5). *"There shall be no more thence an infant of days, nor an
old man that hath not filled his days: for the child shall die an
hundred years old; but the sinner being an hundred years old shall
be accursed. And they shall build houses, and inhabit them; and
they shall plant vineyards, and eat the fruit of them. They shall not
build, and another inhabit; they shall not plant, and another eat:*

for as the days of a tree are the days of my people, and mine elect shall long enjoy the work of their hands. They shall not labour in vain, nor bring forth for trouble; for they are the seed of the blessed of the LORD, and their offspring with them" (Isaiah 65:20-23). It is Israel who is being addressed here by Zechariah, hence the reference to Jerusalem. However in the Millennium many nations will reappear as promised, whilst others will not. God will allocate territories and none will be disadvantaged.

Long ago God reduced the human lifespan to one hundred and twenty years and later to an average of seventy, but in the Millennium Methuselah's record will be broken by millions. However, and here we are reminded that this is not Heaven, the human heart of mortals will still be capable of harbouring rebellion without the intrusion of an external tempter, as we will be reminded in the final section of this chapter. Death will be the exception, but not totally absent (Isaiah 65:20).

IMMORTALS IN THE MILLENNIUM

Some have puzzled as to how mortal and immortal humans will live on the same earth; this is understandable, because it is all so far beyond our experience. We have only one precedent, which is Jesus Christ Himself during the forty days between His resurrection and ascension. Then He would appear or disappear at will, even in locked rooms. He invited Thomas to touch Him to make sure that He was not a ghost, and He shared a meal at the lakeside. And yet nothing He did was in the nature of a stunt; it was all completely natural in His resurrection body. Victorian writer William Kelly says that it was not unlike the way that angels would appear and disappear in the book of Genesis – not a bad comparison, I feel. Jacob became aware in his visionary dream of a stairway or ladder to Heaven; angels, who had this apparently instant access when on God's duty, had their home elsewhere.

Now I must stress that, even among Millenarians or Chiliasts (those who believe in the future Millennium), there is not a complete consensus; I have had to change my own position quite recently here after many years of pondering. I share what I have come to believe is the simplest and most satisfactory explanation, and have many but not all respected commentators to support me.

In the opening verses of John 14, which we quoted earlier, we noted that Jesus said that He was going to prepare a place for us, that He would come again for us, and that where He was going we would forever be with Him. Now what used to puzzle me was that we, the Church, seemed to be going to this lovingly prepared home only for the short period between the Rapture and Coming in Power, when we would vacate it for a thousand years. In such a scheme of things the Old Testament and Tribulation saints would not see it for a very long time!

However we read in Revelation 21: *"And there came unto me one of the seven angels which had the seven vials full of the seven last plagues, and talked with me, saying, Come hither, I will shew thee the bride, the Lamb's wife. And he carried me away in the spirit to a great and high mountain, and shewed me that great city, the holy Jerusalem, descending out of heaven from God, Having the glory of God: and her light was like unto a stone most precious, even like a jasper stone, clear as crystal; And had a wall great and high, and had twelve gates, and at the gates twelve angels, and names written thereon, which are the names of the twelve tribes of the children of Israel..... And the wall of the city had twelve foundations, and in them the names of the twelve apostles of the Lamb...... And I saw no temple therein: for the Lord God Almighty and the Lamb are the temple of it. And the city had no need of the sun, neither of the moon, to shine in it: for the glory of God did lighten it, and the Lamb is the light thereof. And the nations of them which are saved shall walk in the light of it: and the kings of the earth do bring their glory and honour into it. And the gates of it shall not be shut at all by day: for there shall be no night there. And they shall bring the glory and honour of the nations into it (or unto it) And there shall in no wise enter into it any thing that defileth, neither whatsoever worketh abomination, or maketh a lie: but they which are written in the Lamb's book of life"* Revelation 21:9-12,14,22-27. That is a long quote, but an important one. The title Holy City encompasses both the location and its inhabitants.

Now some might react to the idea of this happening at the outset of the Millennium, rather than following it, by pointing out that Revelation 21 opens with the words: *"And I saw a new heaven and a new earth: for the first heaven and the first earth were passed away; and there was no more sea."* In fact the description of the end of the world starts at verse 9 of the previous chapter and continues, I believe, to 22:5. But we have a notable obvious precedent in Isaiah: *"For, behold, I create new heavens and a new earth: and the former shall not be remembered, nor come into mind. But be ye glad and rejoice for ever in that which I create: for, behold, I create Jerusalem a rejoicing, and her people a joy"* (Isaiah 65:17-18). If we miss that important *'But'*, we are left to assume that the remainder of that lovely chapter is about the new Heaven and Earth. But even the most cursory reading demonstrates that it is very different from the sinless state of Heaven. We will say a little more in our short final chapter, but it seems that verses 1 to 8 of Revelation 21 describe what is to happen when this creation has passed away, but that **thereafter** the picture is of the descended home of the resurrected saints throughout the Millennium. Exactly how it will appear or where it will be we cannot say. The kings of the earth bring honour *to* it, rather than *into* it. We will see more of how this can work in the following two sections.

Resurrected saints will have responsibilities and honours awarded according to their faithfulness during this earthy life. Resurrected King David is mentioned several times as being over the house of Israel, with apparently a mortal descendant or Prince (Ezekiel 44:3). His earthly descendant, Zerubbabel is also to have a special place of honour (Haggai 2:23). The twelve apostles are to sit on twelve thrones judging the tribes of Israel (Matthew 19:27-28). Some of the seven congregations of Revelation chapter 2 and 3 are told of future honour for present service, for instance: *"And he that overcometh, and keepeth my works unto the end, to him will I give power over the nations: And he shall rule them with a rod of iron; as the vessels of a potter shall they be broken to shivers: even as I received of my Father"* (Revelation 2:26-27). Now that's not Heaven either, is it?

James and John, not comprehending the full implications of their request, asked: *"Grant unto us that we may sit, one on thy right hand, and the other on thy left hand, in thy glory"*. Jesus replied: *"To sit on my right hand and on my left hand is not mine to give; but it shall be given to them for whom it is prepared"* (Mark 10:37,40 NKJV). That too is about earth, not Heaven. On the night of His betrayal, at that very special Last Supper, Jesus said to the Eleven: *"For I say unto you, I will not drink of the fruit of the vine, until the kingdom of God shall come"* (Luke 22:18). Again, that is not Heaven but the Millennial earth; I keep emphasising this point because far too many think that the world will end with Christ's return. In Matthew 26:29 we learn that He will share that future celebration with His disciples. However Jesus stressed to the Jews that the Millennial Kingdom, described as the Kingdom of God in Mark and Luke but Kingdom of Heaven in Matthew, is by no means only for Jews, as many of them had assumed. Although Jews will indeed have a special status, there will be more Gentiles than Jews! *"I say unto you, That many shall*

*come from the east and west, and shall sit down with Abraham,
and Isaac, and Jacob, in the kingdom of heaven. But the children of
the kingdom shall be cast out into outer darkness: there shall be
weeping and gnashing of teeth"* (Matthew 8:11,12).

The following verses add to our knowledge. Note that there
will be provision for the healing of the nations, something
which will be quite unnecessary in the new creation. *"And
he shewed me a pure river of water of life, clear as crystal, proceeding
out of the throne of God and of the Lamb. In the midst of the street
of it, and on either side of the river, was there the tree of life, which
bare twelve manner of fruits, and yielded her fruit every month:
and the leaves of the tree were for the healing of the nations. And
there shall be no more curse: but the throne of God and of the Lamb
shall be in it; and his servants shall serve him. And they shall see
his face; and his name shall be in their foreheads. And there shall
be no night there; and they need no candle, neither light of the sun;
for the Lord God giveth them light: and they shall reign for ever
and ever* (Revelation 21 and 22:1-5). This New Jerusalem is
apparently to remain a distinct entity, not dependent upon
the sun for light.

CHRIST REIGNING UPON EARTH
In that renowned visitation, Gabriel said to Mary: *"Behold,
thou shalt conceive in thy womb, and bring forth a son, and shalt
call his name JESUS. He shall be great, and shall be called the Son
of the Highest: and the Lord God shall give unto him the throne of
his father David: And he shall reign over the house of Jacob for
ever; and of his kingdom there shall be no end"* (Luke 1:31-33).
That has yet to happen. Jesus at present is seated on His
Father's heavenly throne (Revelation 3:21); this promise will
be fulfilled following His return to earth. Pilate questioned
Jesus about His kingship, and was told by Him: *"My kingdom
is not of this world. If My kingdom were of this world, My servants
would fight, so that I should not be delivered to the Jews; but **now***

My kingdom is not from here." (John 18:36). That little word 'now' is so significant. Just as He did not come to judge two thousand years ago but will one day soon, so He did not come to reign on earth then, but will one wonderful day.

This section and the following one cover the same awesome subject, but we will look at two emphases or aspects. Referring to what is to happen immediately after Christ's Coming in Power, the simple statement is made: *"And the LORD shall be king over all the earth: in that day shall there be one LORD, and his name one"* (Zechariah 14:9). Now within Christianity there is much confusion about this kingship. Outsiders might well come into the average church, sing a few hymns and hear a prayer or two and ask the very reasonable question, "How can God be reigning when the world is in such a mess?" The mighty King Nebuchadnezzar had to learn a very hard lesson about God's sovereignty and His right to intervene in the affairs of men: *"This matter is by the decree of the watchers, and the demand by the word of the holy ones: to the intent that the living may know that the most High ruleth in the kingdom of men, and giveth it to whomsoever he will, and setteth up over it the basest of men".* Later, having learned his lesson, he declared: *"How great are his signs! and how mighty are his wonders! his kingdom is an everlasting kingdom, and his dominion is from generation to generation"* (Daniel 4:3, 17). Nebuchadnezzar had been given an outline of God's plan of the ages as far as the start of the Millennium: *"And in the days of these kings shall the God of heaven set up a kingdom, which shall never be destroyed: and the kingdom shall not be left to other people, but it shall break in pieces and consume all these kingdoms, and it shall stand for ever"* (Daniel 2:44). Jesus Christ is the **rightful** King, and the **coming** King. But as yet He is not the **recognised** King or **accepted** King. One day He will most certainly be.

He will be King of the whole world with His ordained local subordinate king in Israel: *"They shall serve the LORD their God, and David their king, whom I will raise up unto them"* (Jeremiah 30:9). Psalm 72 tells us much of His world-wide reign: *"He shall judge thy people with righteousness, and thy poor with judgment (or justice)..... He shall have dominion also from sea to sea, and from the river unto the ends of the earth..... Yea, all kings shall fall down before him: all nations shall serve him. ..... His name shall endure for ever: his name shall be continued as long as the sun: and men shall be blessed in him: all nations shall call him blessed"* (vv 2,8,11,17). His will be a righteous, just and equable reign. His capital city will be Jerusalem. We will see more in the following section

CHRIST WORSHIPPED UPON EARTH
In formerly Christian countries, it has become acceptable or even fashionable to encourage ancient pagan cultures. Halloween, for instance is regarded with amusement as being harmless fun. God judges nations which forsake His ways; are we not under judgment? In the Millennium nothing other than true worship will be tolerated. This will be no unfair imposition; worship should be from the heart. God's Holy Spirit will be accessible to all. *"For the earth shall be filled with the knowledge of the glory of the LORD, as the waters cover the sea"* (Habbakuk 2:14).

Although Israel and Jerusalem feature prominently in Millennial promises given originally by Hebrew prophets, worship of the Lord Jesus Christ will be obligatory to all nations, and indeed ought then to be natural and spontaneous. *"And many nations shall come, and say, Come, and let us go up to the mountain of the LORD, and to the house of the God of Jacob; and he will teach us of his ways, and we will walk in his paths: for the law shall go forth of Zion, and the word of the LORD from Jerusalem"* (Micah 4:2). *"And it shall be said in that day, Lo, this is our God; we have waited for him, and he will save us: this is the LORD; we have waited for him, we will be glad and rejoice in his salvation"* (Isaiah 25:9). Jews will have a special ministering role: *"Thus saith the LORD of hosts; In those days it shall come to pass, that ten men shall take hold out of all languages of the nations, even shall take hold of the skirt of him that is a Jew, saying, We will go with you: for we have heard that God is with you"* (Zechariah 8:22-23).

There will be a Millennial temple upon earth, but not in the descended Holy City, which will need none: *"And I will shake all nations, and the desire of all nations shall come: and I will fill this house with glory, saith the LORD of hosts. The silver is mine, and the gold is mine, saith the LORD of hosts.The glory of this latter house shall be greater than of the former, saith the LORD of hosts: and in this place will I give peace, saith the LORD of hosts"* (Haggai 2:7-9). At first all will gladly worship. But later, as children are born, who never experienced the Tribulation period, there will apparently be reluctance or even resistance in some, something that will never happen in Heaven: *"And it shall come to pass, that every one that is left of all the nations which came against Jerusalem shall even go up from year to year to worship the King, the LORD of hosts, and to keep the feast of tabernacles. And it shall be, that whoso will not come up of all the families of the earth unto Jerusalem to worship the King, the LORD of hosts, even upon them shall be no rain. And if the family of Egypt go not up, and come not, that have no rain; there shall be the plague, wherewith the LORD will smite the heathen that come not up to keep the feast of tabernacles. This shall be the punishment of Egypt, and the punishment of all nations that come not up to keep the feast of tabernacles"* (Zechariah 14:16-19).

Chapters 40 to 48 of the book of Ezekiel tell us many details of the Millennial Temple, which will be quite different from all previous temples, and of the reallocation of the Promised

Land to the twelve tribes, and much more of the local geography. From Isaiah 2 and Micah 4 we know that it will be in a prominent, elevated place: *"Beautiful for situation, the joy of the whole earth, is mount Zion, on the sides of the north, the city of the great King"* (Psalm 48:2). Unlike the former Jerusalem temples, there will be no veil to separate and no mercy seat, because then Christ's sacrificial death will not be anticipated as needful, but will simply be commemorated as being complete and eternally effective. The veil has been done away with forever.

Ezekiel chapter 43 tells how the glory of the Lord, what was called the Shekinah glory, which was present in the wilderness Tabernacle and Solomon's subsequent Temple (Exodus 40:38), but which departed shortly before Jerusalem's sacking by Nebuchadnezzar (Ezekiel 11:23), will at last return. While every eye will see Jesus Christ at His return, only the immortal saints in the separate Holy City will always be able to see the Lamb face to face (Revelation 22:4). *"And, behold, the glory of the God of Israel came from the way of the east: and his voice was like a noise of many waters: and the earth shined with his glory..... And the glory of the LORD came into the house by the way of the gate whose prospect is toward the east. So the spirit took me up, and brought me into the inner court; and, behold, the glory of the LORD filled the house* (Ezekiel 43:2,4-5). The glory of the Lord appeared in the Tabernacle and first Temple as a pillar of smoke by day and of fire by night; so apparently will it be during the Milllennium: *"And the LORD will create upon every dwelling place of mount Zion, and upon her assemblies, a cloud and smoke by day, and the shining of a flaming fire by night"* (Isaiah 4:5).

THE FINAL CHALLENGE
Long ago Jesus told the Samaritan woman: *"Woman, believe me, the hour cometh, when ye shall neither in this mountain, nor*

yet at Jerusalem, worship the Father..... But the hour cometh, and now is, when the true worshippers shall worship the Father in spirit and in truth: for the Father seeketh such to worship him" (John 4:21,23). And so it is today. The Crusaders, mistakenly thinking that they could buy a ticket to Heaven by pre-empting Jesus' future deliverance, captured and briefly held the city. Even in the Millennium not all will worship in spirit and in truth.

That wonderful kingdom is not to end altogether, but only to end upon earth (I Corinthians 15:24-25). We saw in our last chapter that Satan is to be released after the thousand years. This seems strange until we pause to think that in all that time there will have been no external tempter, and that Christ's benevolent but iron rule will have prevented any rebellion to surface. But those who have been born during the Millennium must make the conscious choice between accepting and rejecting Jesus Christ as personal Saviour. Indeed, every angel and every human has a moral responsibility towards their Creator; salvation will not be automatic. We cannot blame the environment for our relationship with God; even that golden age will not be a guarantee. The testing time will be mercifully short. *"And when the thousand years are expired, Satan shall be loosed out of his prison, And shall go out to deceive the nations which are in the four quarters of the earth, Gog and Magog, to gather them together to battle: the number of whom is as the sand of the sea. And they went up on the breadth of the earth, and compassed the camp of the saints about, and the beloved city: and fire came down from God out of heaven, and devoured them. And the devil that deceived them was cast into the lake of fire and brimstone, where the beast and the false prophet are, and shall be tormented day and night for ever and ever"* Revelation 20:7-10). This is not to be confused with the war of Ezekiel 38 and 39 mentioned in our chapter 3. It seems that it will be the visible earthly

Jerusalem, where God's presence always is, which will be the objective and point of destruction of Satan's hordes. This time there will be no respite for the Devil, and none for his followers.

CHAPTER 7

One Creation Ends, Another Starts

REALITIES BEYOND OUR COMPREHENSION

We now come to realities which are quite beyond our
experience, our comprehension and our ability to imagine.
The only way to describe such things is to compare them
with what we know, so that we can grasp something of their
significance. In view of that statement, we need hardly be
ashamed of not being able to explain more! The Millennium
ends with the last brief rebellion put down and the final
decisions made as to where men and women will spend
eternity. Christ's Kingdom is everlasting, but its time upon
this planet comes at last to an end: *"Then cometh the end, when
he shall have delivered up the kingdom to God, even the Father;
when he shall have put down all rule and all authority and power.
For he must reign, till he hath put all enemies under his feet. The
last enemy that shall be destroyed is death"* (I Corinthians 15:24-
26).

Some think that the earth will be reformed after a complete
clear-out, but I am inclined to agree with those who think
that the whole present visible creation will dissolve: *"But the
heavens and the earth, which are now, by the same word are kept
in store, reserved unto fire against the day of judgment and
perdition of ungodly men"* (II Peter 3:7). *"Lift up your eyes to the
heavens, and look upon the earth beneath: for the heavens shall
vanish away like smoke, and the earth shall wax old like a garment,
and they that dwell therein shall die in like manner: but my*

salvation shall be for ever, and my righteousness shall not be abolished" (Isaiah 51:6). The word 'create' is unambiguous: *"For, behold, I create new heavens and a new earth: and the former shall not be remembered, nor come into mind"* (Isaiah 65:17). Perhaps we cannot help thinking that on that day we will have pangs of regret to see so many happy memories dissolved forever; but think of the unhappy ones!

On the day that I completed this book a leaflet came through my letter box telling me: "You really can live for ever in Paradise on earth." The timing was providential; it allowed me to insert this paragraph. Neither I nor the people who produced the leaflet, so-called Jehovah's Witnesses, can live forever on earth, because this world is due to pass away following the Millennium, as we are about to see from Scripture. They liberally quote Millennial prophecies, giving a superficial impression of orthodoxy. But their gospel is quite different. In the leaflet they quote Luke 23:43, *"You will be with me in Paradise",* but carefully omit the *"today",* which is ruinous to their beliefs, as it emphasises that this was the third day before Jesus' bodily resurrection, which they deny, along with His visible, physical return in power.

THE LAST JUDGMENT
We must now face up to what we may feel is the unpalatable truth of everlasting punishment for those who reject God's salvation. Of course we don't know all about the opportunities that individuals have had, but we do trust in the absolute righteousness of the eternal Judge: *"For the Father judgeth no man, but hath committed all judgment unto the Son"* (John 5:22).

Perhaps the following verses are the gravest words ever committed to print. At the age of fifteen, giving my testimony at a cadet camp, I read them to some of my peers without turning a hair. Now at the age of seventy-six I quote them with fear and trembling for others, though, thanks to God's love, I know that they do not apply to me: *"And I saw a great white throne, and him that sat on it, from whose face the earth and the heaven fled away; and there was found no place for them. And I saw the dead, small and great, stand before God; and the books were opened: and another book was opened, which is the book of life: and the dead were judged out of those things which were written in the books, according to their works. And the sea gave up the dead which were in it; and death and hell delivered up the dead which were in them: and they were judged every man according to their works. And death and hell were cast into the lake of fire. This is the second death. And whosoever was not found written in the book of life was cast into the lake of fire"* (Revelation 20:11-15).

All believers of ages, whether before or after the Flood, before or after Calvary, or before or after the Rapture, will be exempt, because they are redeemed by the blood of the Lamb, and their names are therefore written in the Lamb's Book of Life. We may assume that the mortal bodies of the redeemed of the Millennium will by now have been transformed into immortality, like those of the living Church saints were at the earlier Rapture. Only those whose names are not written there will appear at the awful Great White Throne; but the Lamb's Book of Life will be on show to testify against them and to justify their presence there. Those who appear there will also have been resurrected, though not gloriously, and will stand spirit, soul and body before the all-seeing eyes of their Creator. This is the often conveniently ignored resurrection of the unredeemed, whose conscious souls will have been in Sheol (Hebrew) or Hades (Greek) until this point. In many churches there is a stubborn and growing resistance to the fact of Hell being eternal. If we think about it, there is nothing whatsoever loving about giving people a false assurance of total annihilation following the last judgment, when the Bible declares otherwise. The same language is use to describe the eternal nature of Hell as of Heaven.

We are told that they will be judged according to their works. Works cannot save anybody, but they still count in a way. Believers are rewarded earlier for service to their Saviour (I Corinthians 3:13). In a way which we do not fully understand, works of unbelievers will be taken into account, and for some Hell will be more tolerable than others, perhaps to a much greater degree than we suspect. Only the Lord Jesus Himself talked about it being more tolerable for some (Matthew 11:20-24, Mark 6:11, Luke 10:10-15); perhaps it was too solemn for anyone else to reveal. The amount of data which simple and comparatively novel man-made computers can store solemnises us when we begin to imagine God's data storage resources, far beyond reach of viruses and melt down.

NEW HEAVEN AND EARTH

How can we describe the indescribable? *"As it is written, Eye hath not seen, nor ear heard, neither have entered into the heart of man, the things which God hath prepared for them that love him"* (I Corinthians 2:9). A short summary is found in Revelation 21, which tells us some of the facts which strike a chord with us now: *"And I saw a new heaven and a new earth: for the first heaven and the first earth were passed away; and there was no more sea. And I John saw the holy city, new Jerusalem, coming down from God out of heaven, prepared as a bride adorned for her husband. And I heard a great voice out of heaven saying, Behold, the tabernacle of God is with men, and he will dwell with them, and they shall be his people, and God himself shall be with them, and be their God. And God shall wipe away all tears from their eyes; and there shall be no more death, neither sorrow, nor crying, neither shall there be any more pain: for the former things are passed away. And he that sat upon the throne said, Behold, I make all things new. And he said unto me, Write: for these words are true and faithful. And he said unto me, It is done. I am Alpha and Omega, the beginning and the end. I will give unto him that is athirst of the fountain of the water of life freely. He that overcometh shall inherit all things; and I will be his God, and he shall be my son"* (Revelation 21:1-7).

The earth will have passed away, but, as the word for 'heaven' also applies to the atmosphere and visible universe, we must not conclude that God's Heaven will vanish, because it is from there that the New Jerusalem will descend. We recall reading in John 14:1-3 of the place which Jesus has gone to prepare for us, which immortal humans from their resurrection onwards will inhabit, including throughout the Millennium. It is incorruptible and not of this world; therefore it is not destined to share in this world's destruction. It seems that God will, at the end of the Millennium, withdraw it to allow it to descend again in the new eternal order. Unlike during the Millennium, there will be no old perishable earth below; that will have had seas and other familiar features, whereas the new order will not. We need not think of it as being strange, because nowhere where our risen and glorified Saviour is will seem strange; rather it will be our eternal home.

THE MISCHIEF OF A MISPLACED MILLENNIUM
Much mischief stems from denying, allegorising or misplacing in the scheme of things the Millennial Kingdom. Post-Millennialism, which dates back to the so-called Age of Enlightenment, has had its day. Its claim that the Lord will return only after the Church has made the world fit for His coming sounds hollow indeed in the 21st Century. Amillennialism, the denial of a literal golden age such as we have seen to follow Armageddon, was well established by the end of the 4th Century and helped to promote a variety of

doctrines and practices which led the Church into the Dark Ages. The Reformers failed to eradicate it. Today it takes two forms, namely massive apathy towards predictive prophecy and, in some quarters, militant opposition to the Pre-Millennial Pre-Tribulational teaching that the Lord's Return for His own could happen at any moment.

You have seen for yourself the evidence in the Holy Scriptures for a comprehensive prophetic programme extending for over a thousand years. The direct and indirect consequences of denying its implications result in a number of virtually interdependent distortions, such as:-

- The myth that the Church has forever replaced Israel.
- The lie that Israel has no future in God's plans.
- The misconception that the Church is the new Israel
- The fallacy that the world will end with Armageddon.

Moreover the miraculous element in predictive prophecy is eroded and the Bible is seen as being less authoritative and less inspired in many eyes.

It would be very wrong indeed to accuse all Amillennenialists of Anti-Semitism. However their teaching underpins to varying degrees within the nominal church the following:-

- The denial of the Holy Land as the Promised Land of the Jews.
- Denial of the right of Israel to exist as a nation.
- The encouragement of Palestinian separatism and its right to Jerusalem.
- International marginalisation and boycotting of Israel.
- Active Ant-Semitism.

And those who practise Anti-Semitism can only incur God's wrath. Yet incongruously some who condone it actually dare to seek God's blessing and ask for relief from judgment!

ONLY OPTIONS OPEN

Vulcanologists, environmentalists, agronomists, meteorologists, sociologists and other specialists would regard what the Bible tells us will happen during the coming Tribulation as the natural outcomes of other prophesied events. These prophesied phenomena are in fact much less far-fetched than what the lurid minds of sci-fi writers or film makers might produce. With a little spiritual insight, we perceive that the greatest contrast with science fiction is the immensity of the gulf between God's purity and holiness and the utter depravity and evil of some of the other forces which are unleashed. We then see how in the end-time scenario there emerge more starkly than ever before only two alternatives (1) that of accepting what God at inconceivable cost did in the Person of His Son in bridging that vast gulf and purchasing salvation, and (2) that of remaining in a defiant, rebellious, rejecting state. We find in Scripture a perfect balance of mercy and justice. The consequences of rejecting this mercy occupy the most portentous parts of prophecy, while the endless joys of accepting it are vividly described in scenes transcending human imagination. God has a plan for the future and He has outlined His programme. All is under His control. Those who trust Him as Saviour now will be kept safe, not only when the world's armies are mustering for the Battle of Armageddon, but eternally. If we trust in Him now, our concerns must be for others, because our future is assured.

Were Jesus to return today, would you be ready? We dare not gamble with our precious eternal souls. God does not honour a 'wait and see' policy among those who are confronted with the claims of His Gospel. We have already noticed the grim warning in II Thessalonians 2:8-10 that, when the Church has been called home, Satan's man will appear: *"And then shall that Wicked be revealed, whom the Lord*

One Creation Ends, Another Starts

shall consume with the spirit of his mouth, and shall destroy with the brightness of his coming: Even him, whose coming is after the working of Satan with all power and signs and lying wonders, And with all deceivableness of unrighteousness in them that perish; because they received not the love of the truth, that they might be saved. And for this cause God shall send them strong delusion, that they should believe a lie." For those who have not made a calculated rejection beforehand, it seems that the world-wide preaching of the Gospel of the Kingdom and warnings to repent during the Tribulation Period (Matthew 24:14, Mark 13:10, Revelation 14:6-7), perhaps with unprecedented clarity and urgency in the face of impending doom, will provide an opportunity to turn to Christ and be saved. But to gamble on this beforehand would not only be reckless, but fatal.

Those who are saved in those dreadful coming days when the Dragon is cast to earth will, as we have seen: *"Overcome him by the blood of the Lamb and by the word of their testimony, and they did not love their lives to the death"* (Revelation 12:11). They will be able to face death with equanimity, knowing that their names are safely recorded, because they will not be counted among those *"whose name had not been written from the founding of the world in the book of life of the slain Lamb"* (Revelation 13:8 JND). By an amazing divine miracle, God knew back then the decision you have perhaps yet to make! Forget about the extreme Calvinists who say that you have no initiative in the matter. You do have the initiative and the opportunity, because God first took the initiative and invites you to respond; salvation is conditional upon your response. *"All that the Father giveth me shall come to me; and him that cometh to me I will in no wise cast out"* (John 6:37). Take Him at His word. By a simple act of faith in the Christ who has died for us as our sinbearer, we can fulfil the conditions of John 5:24: *"Verily, verily, I say unto you, He that heareth my word, and believeth on him that sent me, hath everlasting life, and shall not come into condemnation; but is passed from death unto life".*

"I can almost hear his footfall, on the threshold of the door,
And my heart, my heart is longing to be with Him evermore."

An Outline Prophetic Plan

1. The world is not about to end, but the present age could end at any time; individuals can be prepared for this by turning now in faith to the Lord Jesus Christ as their Saviour.

2. This age will end with Jesus Christ raising the bodies of those of the Church Age who have died in faith, taking them to the place in Heaven prepared for them in a glorious incorruptible form; believers still alive on earth will also be caught up and transformed.

3. Earth's darkest hour, which will follow this event, will last for only around seven years, during which the sinister person often referred to as the Antichrist, but better described as the Beast, will appear and take temporary control. Believers will be persecuted pitilessly and many will be martyred. There will be disastrous wars, famines, climate change, earthquakes, disasters, pandemics and terrifying cosmic happenings, all on an unprecedented scale.

4. Even in this dread age there will be many genuine opportunities for people to repent and find God, though with a real risk of incurring the wrath of the Beast and consequently martyrdom.

5. This brief period will end with the Battle of Armageddon, with 'ground zero' in the north of Israel, when Jesus Christ will visibly and physically return to earth in great glory, followed by saints and angels, to overthrow the Beast and

his forces, to bind the Devil for a thousand years utterly beyond reach of mankind.

6. Jesus Christ will conduct an assize likened to a shepherd separating sheep and goats, to determine who among the survivors will be allowed to enter the following peaceful thousand year reign.

7. Jesus Christ will rule for a thousand years in absolute justice with a rod of iron. There will be no tempter and lawlessness will not be permitted; but all people will be required to worship Christ. A shattered environment will be restored.

8. Following this Millennium, this earth and its immediate heavens will vanish for ever, to be replaced by imperishable new earth and heavens. The scrupulously fair final judgment of all unbelievers will take place.

Brief Glossary of Essential Terms

Bold print is used for ease of cross-referencing.

Amillennialism The belief that there will be no literal thousand year rule of Christ upon earth, but rather that the present **Church Age** is the **Millennium**.

Abomination of Desolation A detestable, blasphemous image of the **Beast** which is to be set up in the Jerusalem temple by the **False Prophet**.

Armageddon, Battle of The demon driven concentration of the world's armies to confront God, with disastrous result, at the end of the **Great Tribulation**.

Beast One of Satan's two deputies who will be dominant between the **Rapture** and **Coming in Power**. He will ruthlessly rule an empire which will include the **Promised Land** and perhaps the whole world. He will mercilessly persecute believers. Also frequently referred to, though not in the Bible, as the Antichrist. See also **False Prophet**.

Beginning of Sorrows The first half of the **Tribulation Period**.

Church Age The period from Pentecost (50 days after the Passover when Jesus died as the Lamb of God) to the Rapture.

Coming in Power The visible return of the Lord Jesus Christ as King of Kings and Lord of Lords at the end of the **Great Tribulation** to execute judgment upon Satan, the **Beast**, the **False Prophet** and their armies, and to fulfil everything necessary to usher in the **Millennium**. He will be followed by the armies of **Heaven** – saints and angels.

False Prophet Also described as the Second Beast; this is the evil being who supports and directs worship towards the **Beast**. He will possess miraculous powers and will enforce the **Mark of the Beast**.

Great Tribulation The second half of the **Tribulation Period** and an unprecedented, unrepeatable time of suffering for the world.

Great White Throne The judgment following the **Millennium**, the end of this world and the second resurrection, for the unsaved only – those whose names are not written in the Lamb's Book of Life.

Heaven (1) God's dwelling place, not of this creation. (2) The visible universe or 'starry heavens'. (3) Earth's atmosphere. The souls and spirit of believers awaiting resurrection are with their Lord in Heaven.

Hell Also Gehenna and the Lake of Fire. As yet unoccupied, but eternal. Sheol (Hebrew) and Hades (Greek), the present abode of the souls and spirits of the unbelieving dead is wrongly translated in the A.V. and some creeds as Hell. Before Jesus' resurrection and ascension believers were in a happier part of Sheol.

Heptad Any group of seven. Applied to the seventy groups of seven or 'weeks' of years, 490 years in all, foretold through Gabriel in Daniel 9. The first 69 heptads expired when Jesus was rejected as Messiah. One heptad, constituting the **Tribulation Period** remains to be fulfilled after the **Rapture**, though not necessarily starting at that moment.

Jehovah The Covenant name for God in the Old Testament, rendered as LORD or GOD in capitals in three of the four Bible versions quoted in this book, and left as Jehovah in the JN Darby translation. The Jewish Septuagint scholars who translated the Old Testament into Greek rendered it as *Kurios*, which in turn translates as Lord in the New Testament.

Mark of the Beast A mark, perhaps an implant, to be worn on the right hand or forehead early in the **Great Tribulation**, without which it will be virtually impossible to buy or sell goods. In order to receive it, the holder must swear allegiance to the **Beast**, and thus indirectly to Satan. For this reason those who receive it will place themselves beyond salvation.

Messiah In the Old Testament the promised and longed for Deliverer, who in the New Testament is the Christ, revealed as the **Son of God**. When He first came, many sought only a deliverer from oppression and not from their sins.

Millennium The thousand year righteous rule of Christ on earth following the **Battle of Armageddon**, interpreted literally by Millennialists and either figuratively or loosely by many others. Latin for 1,000 years.

Mystery Babylon A blasphemous religious organisation or false church; guilty of the blood of the martyrs. Historically associated with Rome, but in its final form more likely to be a conglomerate of apostate Christianity and paganism, with its headquarters either at Rome or Babylon. Satan and the **Beast** will make use of it, but will ultimately disown and destroy it as they crave direct worship.

Pre-Millennialism The belief that the Church will be raptured and that Jesus will return to earth before the **Millennium**. Most but not all Pre-Millennialists believe that the **Rapture** will occur before the **Tribulation Period**. Held exclusively by evangelicals and underpinning this book.

Preterism The teaching that most or all end-time promises have already been fulfilled.

Promised Land The area between the Euphrates and the River of Egypt was promised to Abraham and his descendants, narrowed down to those of his grandson Jacob (Israel) in perpetuity; however occupation was to be conditional upon their faithfulness to God's covenants. God still holds the 'title deeds' of the Land. To date it has been fully occupied only during Solomon's reign and briefly during the latter part of David's. The generally accepted River of Egypt is seasonal and flows into the Mediterranean from the north of the Sinai Peninsula, although some think it refers to the Nile.

Rapture The future collective snatching or catching up to meet the Lord in the air of the newly resurrected bodies of the dead in Christ and the translated bodies of the living saints, with onward progress to **Heaven**. From the Latin verb meaning to catch up.

Replacement Theology The teaching that, since their rejection of their **Messiah**, the Jews have no present or future place in God's plans and that the Church has eternally inherited all the blessings and privileges (but apparently not the curses!) accorded to Israel. Has sometimes led to Anti-Semitism.

Seals, Seven Seals of a scroll to be opened in **Heaven** by

Jesus Christ in His offices as the Lamb that had been slain, Lion of the Tribe of Judah and Root of David. Each Seal is a heavenly trigger or authorisation for events on earth during the **Tribulation Period**; these will include the Four Horsemen of the Apocalypse, and will institute two series of seven judgments by sounding Trumpets and pouring out Bowls of Wrath; these take us to the point of Christ's **Coming in Power**.

Son of God Although infinitely beyond our ability to comprehend fully, God is revealed as Triune – Father, Son and Holy Spirit, one God. Perhaps most easily grasped if we remember that each one of us is spirit, soul and body yet a single person, whose elements are temporarily split at death. *"For unto which of the angels said he at any time, Thou art my Son, this day have I begotten thee? And again, I will be to him a Father, and he shall be to me a Son? And again, when he bringeth in the firstbegotten into the world, he saith, And let all the angels of God worship him"* (Hebrews 1:5-6).

Son of Man The title which Jesus applied to Himself as the rejected Messiah, who should suffer, be exalted and return in glory. It does not mean son of *a* man, but indicates that He was born as a Man, when He laid aside His glory but not His Godhood. *"The Word became flesh and dwelt among us"* (John 1:14), after which the Gospel writer, who witnessed His resurrection and ascension, added, *"and we beheld his glory, the glory as of the only begotten of the Father, full of grace and truth"*. As the sinless Son of Man He is the uniquely qualified Judge (John 5:27).The title was also applied to Ezekiel and Daniel when engaged in work concerning the glory of God.

Times of the Gentiles Announced by Daniel in his interpretation of King Nebuchadnezzar's dream and confirmed to be on-going by Jesus Himself in His Olivet

Discourse. A succession of five Gentile empires were to dominate the world around Israel and occupy that Land. These were Babylon, Medo-Persia, Greece and Ancient Rome followed by a long time interval and the final yet future reappearance of Rome as a sort of revived Roman Empire. They end at Christ's Coming in Power.

Tribulation Period   The seven years before Christ's **Coming in Power**. Split into two halves; which are variously described in Scripture as 1,260 days, 3 years, 42 months and 'times, time and half a time'. The first half may be referred to as 'the **Beginning of Sorrows**; the second and more severe half as 'The **Great Tribulation'** or 'Time of Jacob's Trouble. In the Prophets and the Olivet Discourse the Tribulation Period is likened to the two stages of birth pangs. The word 'tribulation' when not pre-fixed by 'the' refers to any period of trial.